Green Beans & Ice Cream

The Remarkable Power of Positive Reinforcement

"It must be realized that there is nothing more difficult to plan, more uncertain of success, or more dangerous to manage than a new order of things…for he who introduces it makes enemies of all those who derived advantage from the old order and finds but lukewarm defenders among those who stand to gain from the new one.

"Such a lukewarm attitude grows partly out of fear of the adversaries and partly from the incredulity of men in general, who actually have no faith in new things until they have been proven by experience."

—Niccolo Machiavelli, circa 1513

Table of Contents

[1] *R+ is a registered trademark of Aubrey Daniels International, Inc. Used with permission*

[1] *R+ is a registered trademark of Aubrey Daniels International, Inc. Used with permission*

Foreword...

Well here it is—my first book.

In the movie that bears his name, Forrest Gump said, "Life is like a box of chocolates." I think my life has proven him to be correct. My early years in business can best be summed up as the proverbial "start-up with a shoe-string budget," "wing and a prayer," and "the school of hard knocks." Many years later, when I started talking about Green Beans and Ice Cream, I had no idea that people around the world would want to hear the message, and that it would resonate so strongly with them. I am humbled that it has touched so many hearts and hope that in some small way it will make a difference for you, too.

While there is a long, long list of people who have inspired and helped me, I respect your patience as my reader and readily acknowledge that we cannot list them all. Nevertheless, just a few of those I wish to thank from my professional world are Aubrey Daniels, Bob Nelson, Gene Owens, Gail Snyder, George Self, Mark and Neil Biteler, Doug Hamilton, Dave Stanley, Vic Anapolle, Ray Miller, Bruce Majors, Diana Linville, Ken Yockey, Larry Beggs, Kenny Sawyer, Barbara Glanz, Leo Inghilleri,

Billy Yarbrough, Max Dover, Lisa Kane, Bob Coleman, Jane Greer, Keith Johanson, Marie Jones, Bob Veazie, Jitu Patel, Faiz Al-Thiga, Ann Lindsey, Tom Hippe, Ron Ellis, Darryl Oscars, Tommy Sides, Rudi Fillingim, Mike Gibney, and Steve Kopecki—I thank all of you for believing in me and for the different perspectives on human behavior that you have helped me to see.

From the bottom of my heart, I thank my mother, Edna, and my father, Bill Sr., for being the two parents that every kid wants to have, and for patiently guiding and mentoring me. I honor my brother, David, and sister, Bonnie, for their hard work alongside me. I thank my wife, Margie, for believing in me when the chips were down. Finally I both commend and thank my two precious daughters, Carli and Daphne, for making our home a cherished place to return to after all those long, hard days, and for letting your daddy get on yet another airplane.

I love you all…

The Little Rebel

It was suppertime, and there they were again:

Green. Slimy. Stringy.

My worst nightmare—yeah, it was green beans all right—again.

By the time I was a four-year-old kid, I had already sampled green beans and concluded they weren't for me. The strings might as well have been wood chips, the way they caught in my throat as I tried to get them down.

Mom was my boss, and I was her newest employee. We had a real labor/management crisis going on. She begged, cajoled and pleaded. *But I was determined not to eat those green beans.*

So I crossed my arms, frowned and pouted, figuring she'd give up and forget about green beans, as she always had in the past.

But this time, Mom had a secret weapon. Now, there was something else on the table besides that dreaded green scourge. "Billy Joe, if you eat your green beans you can have some…"

You guessed it. "Ice cream!"

This sheer stroke of maternal genius changed my behavior forever. In a flash, I saw those green beans, not as an oppressive burden, but as a first-class ticket to that lovely ice cream.

Sure, Mom got what she wanted—a balanced diet for her four-year-old.

And I got ice cream. Pretty cool. (Thanks, Mom. You are the best!) I'm not sure exactly when or how Mom pared back the ice cream, but somehow I came to terms with green beans and accepted them for what they are—pretty healthy and tasty by themselves (oh, Mom learned to buy stringless beans, and that didn't hurt either).

Mom had learned how to *change* my behavior!

2

Why Did He Do That?

Understanding why people do what they do is one of our most daunting challenges. Human behavior has been a subject of discussion since man emerged from the dust. Understanding behavior is a formidable challenge, but it also offers us huge rewards—if we can only crack the code of human behavior change.

Consider a few examples of the power of human behavior:

- **Hitler's focusing the genius of a respected nation on the execution of evil.**

- **The decision to drop the atomic bomb on Japan, an event that brought a proud, powerful country to its knees and dominated international relations for generations to come.**

- **Neil Armstrong's first words and actions on the moon, which captivated the world's imagination: "That's one small step for man, and one giant leap for mankind."**

- **The courageous men and women from the New York City fire department who rushed into the burning Twin Trade towers and gave their lives to save others.**

All of these events included a common factor: human behavior that shaped the world as we know it. After all, what is a country, a family, a school, a business? While the environment, buildings, equipment and furniture are certainly important, it is the tapestry of human behavior that creates what we call "culture."

Culture is made up of many small behaviors and activities.
Sometimes we say that the culture is "toxic" or "nurturing." Many
people assume that culture is what it is, and can never be changed.
At best, they will say that culture change requires a long time.

I beg to differ. Ask Hosni Mubarak (Egypt's strongman before
the Arab Spring melted his power base) how fast culture can change.

Consider the sudden, unexpected collapse of the Soviet Union and
the dismantling of the Berlin Wall.

Consider this common scenario in the
business world:

A president unveils his new plan to turn
around his failing company.

"It won't work, sir," comes the timid
response from his staff. "And why not?"

"The culture here won't support it."

"Culture! What's that? A fuzzy word to hide a lame excuse!" retorts the
frustrated leader.

Sure enough, his plan fails, torpedoed by culture.

The word culture is often hard to define. Here's a definition I like:
"Culture is a pattern of behavior which is encouraged or punished by
the management system over time."

In reality then, to change culture, all we have to do is change

"Culture is a pattern of behavior which is *encouraged or punished* by the management system over time."

behavior. Attitudes follow behavior, just as my attitude about green beans changed over time, after my behavior changed.

But many have been misinformed. An old friend of mine, whom I'd not seen for 20 years, learned about my work in behavior change. In a telephone conversation, he offered up his two cents worth on the subject: "Bill, I remember my professor in psychology to this day. He told me that before you can change behavior, you have to change attitude."

I swallowed hard. He was a good friend, and it had been a long time since we'd talked to each other.

"Crad," I told him, "I hope you won't be upset, but when I see you, I'd really appreciate it if you'd let me tell you why your professor was wrong."

I guess he still likes me, because we went to lunch soon afterward, and I was able to explain to him that to change attitude, you simply have to change behavior. He even asked me to present to a group of 200 company leaders on the subject of positive reinforcement and behavior change!

No matter whether you are a parent, husband, wife, teacher, boss, supervisor, professor, cop, or anything else in life, what you often want from the people around you is the same thing:

BEHAVIOR CHANGE.

**RESULTS ARE THE DESSERT...
BEHAVIORS ARE THE INGREDIENTS.**

BEHAVIORS   RESULT

You want more production, quality, safety and customer service from your employees; better test scores, homework and study habits from your students; cleaner rooms and better grades from your kids. To get more from people, we need behavior change.

Everything we observe can be broken down into behaviors, activities, results and culture. If culture is Beethoven's Fifth Symphony, then every note from every instrument can be likened to a behavior.

Results are achieved by a myriad of behaviors. Think of your favorite dessert. That dessert is the result. But the sugar, flour, butter and other items that make up the dessert are behaviors. When we get the behaviors right, we can cook up some amazing results!

Culture, like a dessert, can be toxic or nurturing.

There's nothing like luscious banana pudding to add warmth and flavor to a meal. But a notorious husband-killer in North Carolina—known as the Black Widow—used banana pudding laced with arsenic to do away with her spouses.

So how do we achieve that nurturing culture?

Can we really navigate the murky world of the human mind?

B. F. Skinner, American behaviorist, social philosopher and poet, once wrote, "Thoughts are behaviors we haven't learned to observe yet."

Until technology allows it, you can't see inside my mind, and I can't see inside yours either. This "black hole" of human logic means that *if we believe attitude must change before behavior, then we will be waiting a very, very long time to see any measurable difference in human performance.* Just ask the Marlboro man how many years he read the Surgeon General's warning printed on every pack of cigarettes he smoked. Did those produce behavior change in him? It was not until he was in the hospital, terminally ill with cancer that his attitude about smoking finally changed. Powerful consequences had forever changed his life, his behavior, and finally, his attitude toward smoking.

Since the complex world of human thought and attitude is at present not easily read, we need another tool to understand human behavior, one that we can implement easily in today's business world.

That tool has existed for more than 70 years. It's a science called "behavioral analysis."

Using some simple and easy tools, we can crack the code that reveals why people do what they do. And we can empower ourselves and others to achieve performance we never thought possible.

This book is devoted to helping you do just that . . .

Changing Attitudes and Self-Motivation

"Manipulating behavior by offering rewards, while a sound approach for training the family pet, can never bring quality to the workplace."

–Alfie Kohn, PhD

Applause bursts out spontaneously from a crowd delighted by the band's performance.

A coach shares a high-five with the player who wins the game.

A baby's first steps are applauded by Mom and Dad.

As hard as Alfie Kohn, Daniel Pink, and others may try to persuade us that external praise and positive feedback are wrong, their arguments do not jibe with the reality of life.

We need positive reinforcement. We cherish feedback confirming that our contributions matter and that we have made a difference in the world around us. Aubrey Daniels has coined a great name for this: R+®. From now on in this book, when you see the abbreviation "R+," you'll know that I am referring to positive reinforcement (of behavior), the most powerful tool on the planet for increasing human performance.

Positive Reinforcement

Butterfly Kisses

"I know the cake looks funny, Daddy, but I sure tried." In this short line from "Butterfly Kisses," a song written by Bob Carlisle and Randy Thomas, a little girl reaches out for her father's approval (positive feedback) to be sure he sees her effort, and he appreciates it.

Bob Nelson's book, *1001 Ways to Reward Your Employees*, reports that of the key drivers of employee happiness and engagement, a recurring top need was, "I am able to make a difference at work" and "My manager has recognized me recently for what I do."

Like the little girl in "Butterfly Kisses," people need to receive feedback from their leaders confirming that their work has value, and they are keenly aware of the presence of this feedback, or the lack thereof.

SELF-REINFORCEMENT IS A VERY POWERFUL **FORM OF R+**

As we pass through a murky, chaotic, ever-changing world, we are anchored by that first "A" from our teacher; that first "Good Citizen" award certificate; that first knowledge that we came, we saw, and we made a positive difference.

Self-reinforcement is a very powerful form of R+ (assuming you aren't suffering from depression).

As my good friend Leo Inghilleri—a highly regarded consultant in the service and hospitality industry—once said, *"The problem with highly self-motivated people is that they tend to assume everyone else is just like them."*

Often, presidents and leaders of companies have very high levels of self-R+ around work ethic. When they are told that their employees need R+ to ensure that they continue to perform at their best, their response is often, "But nobody did that for me, so why should I do it for others?"

So often they don't realize that someone *did* do this for them—a teacher, a parent, a mentor, who gave them positive reinforcement early on.

Does Punishment Really Work?

"When it's game time, it's pain time, baby."

—**Terrible Terry Tate,** *Reebok Super Bowl commercial*

Does punishment really change behavior? In an award-winning Super Bowl commercial, Reebok poked fun at "tough guy" management styles.

"When we asked Reebok to help us improve office productivity, we had no clue how effective their methods would be," says the CEO in the commercial.

Next we see employees goofing off on their jobs, only to be tackled, mauled and screamed at by Terrible Terry Tate, the big, bad football player: "When it's game time, it's pain time!" "In fact, we wish Reebok had sent us ten Terry Tates," the smiling CEO says.

As funny as this clip is, it rings all too true for many of us. ***Does punishment really work over the long haul?***

Against his will, Terry Tate is finally sent on vacation, where he spurs the lackluster hotel staff to unprecedented customer service.

But while he is gone, what happens back at his home office? Margaritaville parties and loss of performance.

While the cat's away, the mice will play. Terry returns to work, realizing that behavior change lasts only as long as he is standing there holding the stick.

To watch the video, visit
www.powerofpositivereinforcement.com

The Wasp and the Hard Hat

In London, four workers are building a brick wall, all wearing their hard hats, as required. Out of nowhere, a wasp flies under one man's hat. The worker quickly doffs the hat. Around the corner comes his boss, who yells, "If you don't put your hard hat on, you're off the project!"

Embarrassed, the red-faced worker puts his hard hat on, while his buddies laugh at him. Convinced that his negative methods have changed behavior, the boss marches off. The supervisor, you see, has just received R+ for screaming at people (because the worker put his hard hat on) and so he repeats the behavior with renewed fervor.

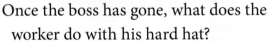

Once the boss has gone, what does the worker do with his hard hat?

You guessed it. He takes it off.

What do we learn from this vignette?

Initially, the worker changed his behavior to avoid punishment from his boss. The boss, therefore, is convinced that punishment and negative reinforcement "work," since the worker changed behavior. *Negative reinforcement produces a temporary shift in behavior (just enough to avoid the pain), which is quickly followed by a reversion to a lower level of performance once the bully has gone.*

Once the manager is gone, the worker shows who the real "boss" is when the hard hat comes back off.

Punishment and negative or "Leave Alone/Zap" managers get behavior change only when they are there holding the stick. In his book, *The One Minute Manager*, Ken Blanchard coined the term "Leave Alone/Zap" to describe a management style in which supervisors leave the workers alone and say nothing when they are doing the job well, and then zap them when they make a mistake.

This same scenario plays out time after time in schools, workplaces—and in families.

"Set the table!"

The young girl grudgingly stops her homework assignment to set the table for dinner.

"Clean your room!"

With a sigh, she heads off to clean her room.

We often tend to use negative reinforcement because we believe it to be the most effective.

"Yes sir, Sir!"

But when we leave, what do people do?

Are the rooms really clean? Is the homework truly done? Are the hard hats on or off? Is the class quiet or rowdy?

People Don't Leave Companies; They Leave Managers

People don't leave a company; they leave their manager, as the study described below showed:

"Many workers feel stressed out, undervalued and dissatisfied with their job," according to a survey by the American Psychological Association. Conducted online, the survey found that 36 percent of the workforce experiences job stress regularly. Although nearly half of respondents cited low salary as having a significant impact on their stress levels, other factors commonly cited included lack of opportunities for advancement (43 percent), heavy workload (43 percent), unrealistic job expectations (40 percent) and long hours (39 percent). Slightly more than one-half of workers reported feeling valued on the job, while nearly one-third reported they intend to seek employment elsewhere in the coming year."

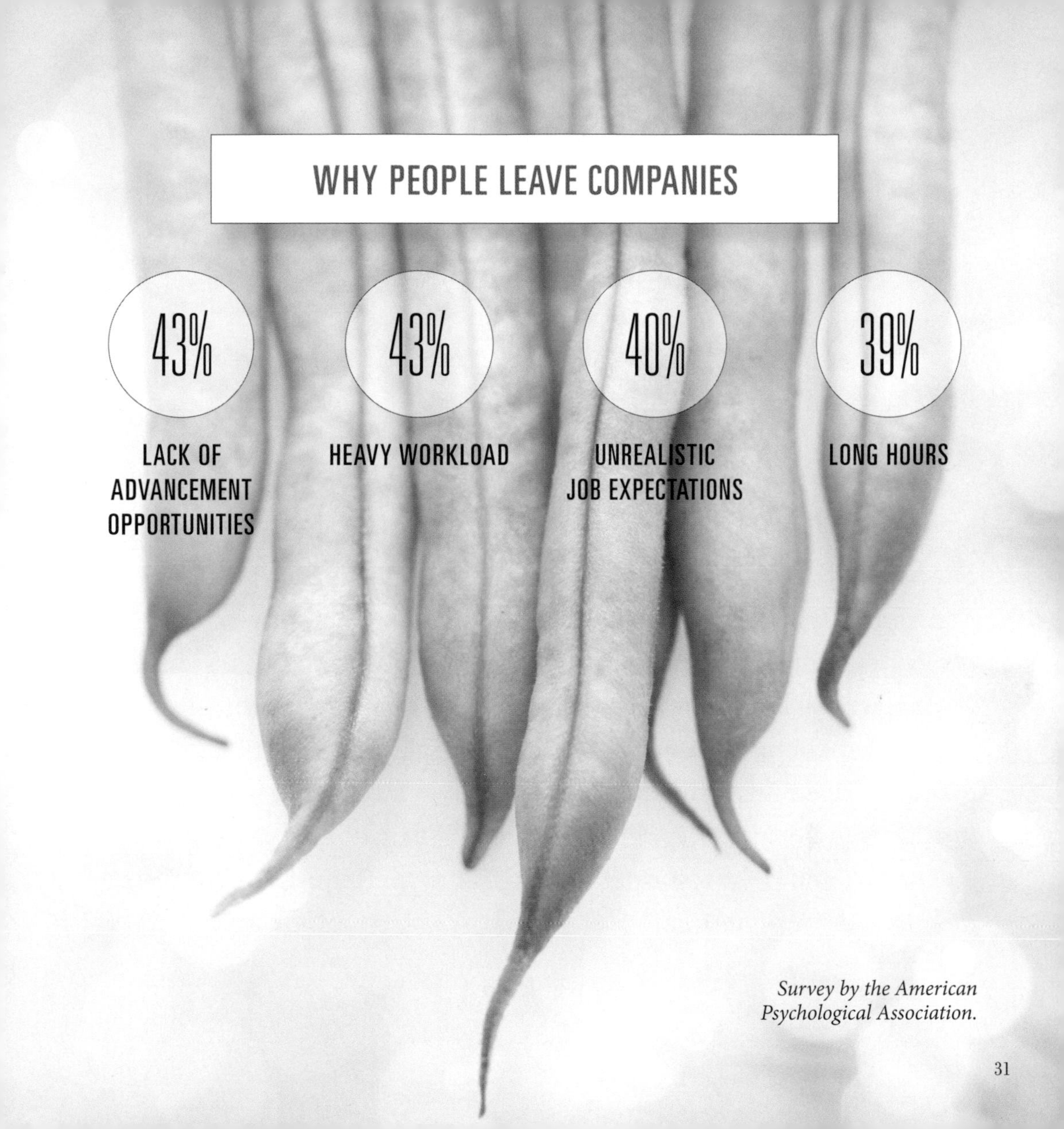

WHY PEOPLE LEAVE COMPANIES

43%
LACK OF
ADVANCEMENT
OPPORTUNITIES

43%
HEAVY WORKLOAD

40%
UNREALISTIC
JOB EXPECTATIONS

39%
LONG HOURS

*Survey by the American
Psychological Association.*

The only bone I have to pick with this survey is that the researchers did not include questions about the lack or presence of R+ in their assessment. It's safe to conclude that lack of R+ is the undercurrent "master problem" driving this employee disengagement.

An Australian CEO lamented to me that he had designed the perfect recognition solution, but none of his managers used it.

Sadly, he had never given anything but punishment and negative reinforcement to his direct reports, which like some other unpleasant things, tends to continue rolling downhill.

Does punishment change behavior? Absolutely.

But the behavior change is short-lived and it fades as quickly as the punisher's dark shadow leaves the room. And managers who choose punishment as their tool of choice have only one option to change behavior—more severe levels of punishment (curt remarks, reprimands, yelling, written warnings, docking of pay, suspension, dismissal).

A classic example is the collection of internal memos written by the owner of Tiger Oil during the 1970s. The owner becomes increasingly insulting and demeaning to his workforce. You can see that he has lost all control, and so he resorts to louder and more frequent threats. Such memos today would prompt a string of lawsuits, but they were "part of the job" when I started my career in the late 1970s and early 1980s.

Read the memos by visiting www.powerofpositivereinforcement.com and clicking on "Diary of a Punisher."

Punishers get exactly what they intend as long as they are standing by to deliver more punishment; the problem is that they have no clue about all the performance—or non-performance—going on in their absence.

The bottom line: you can't punish a team into winning the Super Bowl.

Or, as Bob Nelson, best-selling author and motivational speaker, expressed it, *"You get the best results by creating a fire within people, not by lighting a fire under them."*

THE BOTTOM LINE:

You can't punish a team into winning the Super Bowl.

5

The Church of Here and Now

To get an understanding of consequences and how they drive our behavior, consider the everyday light switch on a wall. When you flip up the switch, at least 99.9 percent of the time the lights will come on. That is an immediate consequence of flipping the switch.

Positive consequences cause you and me to repeat that behavior again and again. We now flip light switches without even having to think about them. We are on "auto-pilot" for this behavior.

punishment & penalty

VERSUS

positive reinforcement

On the other hand, if you flip up a light switch and you get a nasty shock…then those negative and immediate consequences shut down or punish the behavior of flipping light switches. So, when it comes to behavior, people attend the Church of the Here and Now.

Behavioral science also focuses on punishment and penalty, which are all unpleasant. They too will shut down or decrease behavior. In this book, I am focusing on the unique power of positive reinforcement, which blows the doors off all the other kinds of consequences when it comes to attaining human performance improvement.

Volkswagen sponsored an intriguing study of how positive consequences alter human behavior.

To watch the video, visit
www.powerofpositivereinforcement.com
and click the Piano Stairs link

6

Why Does R+ Work?

"There are two things people want more than money: recognition and praise."

—**Mary Kay Ash**, *founder of Mary Kay Cosmetics, Inc.*

Donna was a new manager struggling to get her 300 highway-construction workers to comply with a new company safety rule: wearing a hard hat at all times. She'd done more than her share of yelling and screaming, trying to get compliance with the new rule. Terry Tate would have been proud. Only nobody was taking her seriously.

"Why don't you try some R+?" I asked her. She agreed to give it a shot, and so I sent her my "R+ Care Package," which consisted of a big cooler chest that I felt sure any construction worker would appreciate.

The next day she showed up unexpectedly at a construction site. Following my suggestion, she singled out the only worker who was demonstrating the desired behavior.

Of the 17 guys on the project, only the newest employee was wearing a hard hat (apparently nobody had yet told him that wearing his hard hat was uncool).

Donna walked over to the new employee in front of everyone, while she ignored those who were not wearing their protective gear. She publicly thanked him (that was a little risky but it worked out well this time) for wearing his hard hat, telling him, "Joe, I really appreciate your taking safety seriously. I sometimes lie awake at night worried that one of you won't go home to your family safely, and your taking the time to follow our new safety rule means a lot to me. This gift is for you."

As the 16 rough, weathered construction workers watched, Donna presented the cooler chest to Joe. He responded, "Thanks, Donna! I've never won anything in my whole life, and nobody in safety has ever told me I did something right."

Now the 16 other construction workers asked Donna a question, ***"Where's our cooler chest?"***

"Well guys, where are your hard hats? Maybe during my next safety audit, if I see you with your hard hats on, then we'll talk about cooler chests."

The impact on the other employees was immediate and powerful. On the next trip to the site, Donna was greeted by the entire crew smiling at her and pointing at their hard hats. Donna followed my advice and presented each one with a cooler chest and sincere positive feedback.

R+
works!

Blinded by the Light

It's 1927, and we're at the Hawthorne Works, a factory in Cicero, Illinois. A small group of women have been selected to participate in a unique study to see how lighting affects their productivity. The engineers doing the study are closely monitoring them. They want to see if dimming the lights will affect their productivity. The first week of the study, the researchers lower the lights by 10 percent, and they track the productivity of the team. Amazingly, production increases. The next week, they dim the lights again, and—voilà!—production increases. During the entire time, the workers receive feedback on the number of parts they are producing. This process goes on for a time, with the room getting ever darker and productivity going onward and upward, until it's so dark that the poor ladies can barely see.

The researchers decide to return the lights to full strength, expecting to erase their previous productivity gains, only to find that when the lights are returned to the original setting, productivity increases again.

The researchers reach an astounding conclusion: Lighting has no effect on worker productivity.

What produced the effect? The fact that workers received feedback on their performance as well as autonomy in making work decisions (in later experiments the workers could vote on the length of the work day, the frequency and duration of breaks, and so on). All of this somehow produced what today is known as the "Hawthorne Effect."

Feedback + Autonomy = "Hawthorne Effect."

Why Cash Isn't King

In his 1959 book, *The Motivation to Work*, Dr. Frederick Herzberg explained that the two greatest drivers of employee satisfaction are recognition and achievement, while money ranks a distant sixth place as a satisfier. Perhaps even more fascinating is that money did rank number one as a source of worker disengagement and unhappiness. Unfair pay erodes trust in leadership and decreases performance.

Then, in 1996, Bob Nelson conducted a number of surveys to discover *that the most powerful driver of employee satisfaction and engagement isn't money; it's R+.* Money again ranked a distant fifth place as a satisfier. Sadly, more than 68 percent of all workers have never heard the words "Thank you" from their bosses.

Nelson next interviewed the managers of those same employees to see what they believed would motivate their people. Money was their number-one response. Nearly all of those leaders felt that positive reinforcement and feedback would have little or no impact on worker behavior and performance.

68%
NEVER HEARD "THANK YOU"

The key takeaway from the Nelson study is that there is a huge disconnect between what workers say they want and what managers think they want. Managers see money as the answer, while workers say R+ is more important.

Perhaps what sums it up best is this story, reportedly told during an exit interview with a highly paid attorney, who quit her job to become a waitress. During the interview, she was asked why she had chosen to take a pay cut of more than $100,000 per year to become a waitress.

"I'll be honest," she said. "My boss says something 100 percent of the time when I make a mistake. And when I put forth extra effort, he says nothing 99 percent of the time. At least when I put the customer's breakfast on the table I'll get a 'Thank you.'"

Her manager's style is a classic. In my experience, more than 95 percent of leaders today are using that style without even being aware it has a name: *Leave Alone/Zap management.*

Why do so many managers hesitate to use R+?

Perhaps the fear is that if we commend workers for work well done, it will encourage them to ask for pay raises (which is punishing for the managers).

In the book, *How Starbucks Saved My Life*, author Michael Gates Gill recounts a memo sent during the 1960s to all the managers of the J. Walter Thompson (JWT) ad agency. The memo ordered JWT managers: **"Never positively recognize employees in writing, since they could use this against the company if they are fired."**

Now, most managers think they do a great job at recognizing their employees and believe that a culture of R+ exists in their company.

"Come visit our company and you'll see, Bill! We just finished a week-long, employee-appreciation celebration. We took all the employees out for a full day at a local amusement park and bought them a nice dinner."

While I applaud the intention of this celebration, I can tell you without a doubt that such events do not drive better employee performance. In fact, they punish your outstanding workers, and reward your worst ones. (See Chapter 11: "Cave People: One Size Does Not Fit All.")

Another touching story concerns Norman the Doorman, who made a difference for me during a trip to the El Conquistador Resort in Puerto Rico.

To view that story, visit
www.powerofpositivereinforcement.com

There is a huge disconnect between *what workers say* they want and *what managers think* they want.

Who Killed the Work Ethic?

"What's up with these young people? Where's their work ethic?"

—Baby Boomer manager

W hy don't people pay their dues, the way we did when we first started out?

Post-Depression-era workers were the best. They could be used and abused and would still show up for work the next day, remembering the bread lines and unemployment of their formative childhood years.

That generation has, for the most part, retired.

In their place is a generation of "Latchkey Kids" who remember Mom and Dad being gone a lot.

In the book, *Work with Me*, authors Debra S. Magnuson and Lora S. Alexander explain the generational differences between the workers of the Great Depression era, the Baby Boomers, and their kids and grandkids known as Gen X and Gen Y.

Boomers brought much of the same work ethic to the job that their Depression-era parents did, but they also enjoyed the prosperity of the post-World War II economy. With both Mom and Dad working, most Gen X and Gen Y kids were raised by Nintendo.

One Gen X says, "I watched both of my Baby Boomer parents drag in tired at 8 p.m. from working all day at their jobs. I'll never do that to my kids."

Ever played Nintendo? I have. It's great fun. You do something, you get R+. You do something else, and you get R+. In short, you get positive feedback and positive reinforcement hundreds of times per minute.

BOOMERS

GEN X

GEN Y

Now, if you were reared as a Latchkey Gen X or Gen Y kid on a steady diet of hundreds of R+ per minute, hour after hour every day, how do you think you'd react to an "old-school, my-way-or-the-highway, sink-or-swim" management style?

You might expect just a little conflict between the four generations of American workers. And that is precisely why the older workers often sigh, roll their eyes, and ask this question about Gen X and Gen Y workers, "Who killed the work ethic?"

Managers have ignored great performance for so long that people have become cynical, and the balance of power has shifted toward the worker.

R+
EXAMPLE

Employee engagement is the passionate goal of many managers now and rightly so. A study by Towers Perrin (now Towers Watson), a professional services firm specializing in human-resources and financial-services consulting, found employee

IN SHORT, YOU GET POSITIVE FEEDBACK AND POSITIVE REINFORCEMENT HUNDREDS OF TIMES PER MINUTE.

engagement to be a key driver of every measure of financial success.

The study also showed that the actions of management drive employee engagement, or result in its absence. If superior performance isn't reinforced, people will stop delivering. Maybe that's why fewer than 15 percent of employees today are engaged in their work.

I remember one employee who will always be a hero in my book. When I first started working for my father's company, I was in the shipping department (you name it, I did it, no questions asked).

One day, I decided to extend our concrete drive for our receiving area by pouring the concrete myself. Now, the fact that I had never poured concrete before never fazed me. I had read the "how-to" book, and I was ready to lay concrete.

The concrete truck pulled up. It was July—a horribly hot, high noon in South Carolina. The harder I worked that concrete, the faster it set up. I marvel today at how hard my heart beat as I worked. It's a miracle I didn't pass out.

But it was no use. I had concrete setting up hard, and I couldn't work it out fast enough…until that brown UPS truck rolled up with Mac Robinson, the driver for our route. I knew Mac had a lot to do. I knew that UPS gave drivers a quota of stops and that pushed them pretty hard. So when Mac got out of his truck and started helping me work the concrete, I became forever a UPS customer. We laid the concrete that day, with only a few waves and wrinkles that I still smile at as I pass that driveway some 30 years later.

Did Mac face some possible negative consequences for helping me out? I'm sure he did. His boss wasn't on the truck to see my plight. But Mac was an engaged employee, if ever there was one. I will never forget him or his company.

"Will you paint the wall please?"

Leonardo Inghilleri is one of the key people who helped Horst Schulze make the Ritz Carlton a legend in customer service. Leo teaches new employees that the guest experience can either be a plain, white wall, or a masterpiece like the ceiling of the Sistine Chapel. While both surfaces are painted, one is light years beyond the other. Each interaction with a guest at the Ritz Carlton is like a brushstroke in the master painting.

So, Leo tells his staff, no matter what you do, you are helping paint that picture. This connection with the mission helps Leo's new Capella Hotels create that masterpiece experience.

The Death of a Work Ethic

In his book, *How Starbucks Saved My Life,* Michael Gates Gill, a son of privilege, tells how he prided himself on his exalted progression from boarding school through Yale University and into a lofty career with J. Walter Thompson, one of the world's most prestigious advertising agencies.

As he moved through this rarefied environment, he often looked down on people less fortunate, and conveniently labeled them "under-performers."

Then, out of the blue, Gill lost his job, wealth and family. Then he learned he had a brain tumor. Without health insurance, he desperately sought a job at Starbucks as a last resort.

It became the best job of his life. Here, he began to embrace diversity, and learned to treat others as he would like to be treated.

Gill recalled that at J. Walter Thompson, he had learned that to succeed, he had to cater to his client's every whim.

One of his clients was Ford Motor Company. On Christmas day, while his little children were unwrapping presents, Ford executives insisted that he leave his family immediately for a video shoot. The kids cried and begged him to stay.

He left.

Behold, the Company Man!

Gill gave his all to the agency—until J. Walter Thompson needed a more youthful staff. Then, Gill was fired.

At JWT, the rewards were few, and far between. The expectations were high. Self-motivation and pride carried the day.

I wonder how Gill's children would act if they went to work for JWT?

Would they leave their children crying as he did, simply to meet a client's needs?

Would the intrinsic value of achieving great work make them sacrifice their children and marriages at the helm of success?

I doubt it. Thank goodness for "work/life balance."

As a final thought, I would like to quote Aubrey Daniels, who said to me one day...

"We are all guilty of killing the work ethic, because of our failure as leaders to deliver R+ for desired performance. Who killed the work ethic? We all did."

10

Daughter-of-the-Month

While surveying the employees of one of the top luxury hotel firms in the world, I met Rose, a delightful lady. Rose was in a focus group I held with some of the hotel employees. I asked her how many times she'd been positively reinforced for something done well during her three years of employment at the hotel.

Her eyes narrowed as she searched her memory.

"Only once, when I was voted 'Best Customer Service Employee-of-the-Year,'" she replied.

"Why?" I asked.

"I don't know," she mused. "They never told me. Maybe it was a survey or something? But the worst part was how they surprised me in front of my peers and told them I was the best, and they weren't. Now two of those ladies won't speak to me."

Rose concluded: "It was the worst day of my life!" I call this syndrome "Why them? Why not me?"

Rose was singled out for praise at the expense of her coworkers. So they singled her out for punishment. ***In Australia and New Zealand they describe this as the "Tall Poppy" syndrome, meaning that the tallest poppy in the bunch inevitably gets cut down to size.***

For this very reason, and others, Employee-of-the-Month programs are bad news. Any time you pit one employee against all the others, you have a recipe for disaster. Nobody wants to be seen as the "teacher's pet." To make matters worse, publicly recognizing individuals in front of their peers is a surefire way to erode workplace morale and team spirit.

I have two daughters, Daphne and Carli.

What if I pop in one day from a business trip and line them up and say, "Hey Carli, give Daphne a round of applause, 'cause she's Daughter-of-the-Month, and **you're not.**"

How's that going to go over?

That's precisely what we do with our employees through Employee-of-the-Month programs and other dumb ideas.

11

Cave People: One Size Does Not Fit All

"We do a great job at employee recognition," said the Human Resource manager at a large hospital.

"That's good to know," I said. "How do you go about recognizing great performers?"

"Well, we do a picnic quarterly and select the Employee-of-the-Quarter for each department. Then there's our year-end Christmas party, where we choose an Employee-of-the-Year," she replied.

"How is that working for you?" I asked. "Have you had a positive impact on statistics indicating the satisfaction of your employees and patients? Can you measure and quantify your employee engagement? Did your system really change anybody's behavior?"

She glared back at me in silence. Apparently I had hit a nerve. I had a pretty good idea that this meeting was over.

Oops, I think I did it again. I felt kind of bad for being too direct. It appeared that my honesty had gotten me in trouble yet another time.

But in fact, this company was heavily entrenched in "one-size-fits-all" recognition, which does more harm than good.

By now, if you've read Chapter 10: "Daughter-of-the-Month," you understand clearly why an Employee-of-the-Month, of-the-Quarter, or of-the-Year is a bad idea.

Any time we set up one employee to win at the expense of everyone else, we have given our workplace culture a suicide pill. Competition is what we do in the marketplace, not what we do with our coworkers. Our team rises and falls based on the team's achievements.

Most managers have seen the problems inherent in the "Employee-of-the-Month" approach, and so they've swung the recognition pendulum to the opposite extreme: one-size-fits-all. Too bad these managers skip right over the little sweet spot in the middle that I call "behavior-based recognition."

In "one-size-fits-all" cultures, everybody gets exactly the same thing, whether deservedly or not. You get the same barbecue dinner as I do, despite the fact that you may contribute three times the value to the organization that I do.

Google garnered a lot of negative publicity when it granted a "one-size-fits-all" 10 percent pay raise to every worker in the company,

One size does not fit all

regardless of the individual's contributions. But let's not just pick on Google; almost every company in the world has a pay system with a huge Achilles heel. People (for the most part) get paid to show up at work. Their pay is not tied to their performance or to the viability of their company's product in the marketplace.

We need to recognize the distinction between R+ and the one-size-fits-all approach. *If you're providing positive feedback, reinforcement, recognition, and rewards that result in an increase in the behavior you want, that's R+.* If your program results in a drop in the behavior you want, it's punishment.

So our well-meaning managers have bestowed on their workers a plethora of picnics, barbecues, T-shirt giveaways and endless other celebrations to commemorate safety, sales, quality and other milestones. In these systems, usually a lagging indicator (result) is rewarded and, in the case of safety, we sometimes see the bad effects of injury-suppression, hiding, under-reporting and the like.

This Pandora's Box of bad side effects is one reason that the behavioral community often argues against incentive systems.

"Hey, the one-size-fits-all method is at least better than Employee-of-the-Month method," says the manager.

But is it really? Not in my book. Here's why:

As I've traveled the world speaking, I've used CAVE People to explain why one size does not fit all.

Everywhere I've been, every manager has employees who are CAVE People. I'll bet you have some too.

What's a CAVE person?

My good friend Kenny Sawyer says they are "Citizens Against Virtually Everything."

They whine and complain. They sleep through training meetings. They break the safety rules and drag down your team. They insult your clients and bring your customer satisfaction scores down.

Thank goodness, you also have people who are hard workers—those above-and-beyond people who value their jobs and deliver safe, quality products or guest experiences.

So you have three distinct groups in every culture:

1. High Performers,
2. Average Performers, and
3. CAVE People.

Given this cross-section of the average workforce—High Performers, Average Performers, and CAVE people—how have we attempted to motivate and reward them?

We've used one-size-fits-all reward systems, which go kind of like this:

"Er, excuse me folks; we would like to recognize your performance this past quarter.

"Now, I know that you High Performers have done everything we've asked of you, and a whole lot more.

High Performers   Average Performers   CAVE People

"You CAVE people have slept through every training meeting, broken every safety rule, and missed every deadline we've given you.

"And you average folks, well, what can I say? Thanks for being average."

Now the manager holds a card over his head.

"So, in honor of our team achievements, we're awarding everybody a $100 gift card, and we're going to have a picnic this Saturday, plus a free T-shirt if you show up. Great job people!"

Hold on. Wait a second.

If you adopted this one-size-fits-all method, did you just positively reinforce your high performers, or did you punish them? (Hint: the answer starts with P.)

Let's pretend that you are one of the high performers and I'm a CAVE person working in the cubicle next to you—close enough for each of us to know which role the other fits.

Now suppose that, during "Employee Happiness Day," you happen to be in the steak dinner line, filling up your plate, and I'm right behind you. You think about all the effort you made to help improve performance, and all the things I didn't do.

Then you notice that my steak is just as big as yours.
How does that make you feel? (punished, right?)

So, when you use one-size-fits-all systems, you punish your best workers.

How about the CAVE people? Did you just reinforce their bad behavior?

Yep, you sure did.

You effectively said, "Hey go out and take more shortcuts, break more rules, sleep through more training, and you will be rewarded just as much as our High Performers."

And your Average Performers will actually be encouraged to become CAVE people, thinking, "It does no good to work hard around here. Nobody will notice anyway. Look at those poor High Performer guys. What suckers they are!"

The problem with one-size-fits-all recognition is clear.

Yet, the practice is repeated day in, day out, at millions of companies around the world, in the form of picnics, profit-sharing, gain-sharing, goal-sharing, and the like.

Does it improve performance? No.

So my advice to anyone doing "Employee-of-the-Month" or "One-Size-Fits-All" is to take a hard look at what you're doing and find a strategy linked to performance improvement, on a fair but unequal basis, to everyone.

This means practicing R+: the reinforcement of the behaviors that drive the results you seek.

To achieve the results you want, you need your team to focus on behavior.

"Business Is Behavior."

—Aubrey Daniels

Business leaders today share a common dream: to improve business performance and increase profits. In short, great leaders are always in search of better results.

To change our results, we have to change the behaviors of our people. In my "Green Beans & Ice Cream" sessions with managers, we talk a lot about what makes a great leader. The usual responses are integrity, honesty, dependability, courage, decisiveness and the like. Every one of these qualities is important.

But there is one leadership quality that everyone overlooks, and in my book, it is the most important.

The way I discovered it was during a chat with Eric Schwartz, who worked, at the time, in city government in Fresno, California.

"Bill, I was amazed at how my supervisors rejected the idea that employees needed R+," he said. "They told me that all we needed to do was to give people a paycheck. I looked them dead in the eye and told them this: If all it takes is a paycheck to get great safety, quality and productivity, what do we need you supervisors for?"

I couldn't have said it better, Eric.

What Eric alluded to was the number one trait of great leaders—the ability to change the behavior of others.

Think about it: If people were going to give us their absolute best safety, quality, sales, production and customer service automatically, then most managers would be out of a job.

> TO CHANGE OUR
> **RESULTS,**
> WE HAVE TO
> CHANGE THE
> **BEHAVIORS**
> OF OUR PEOPLE.

Your success as a leader depends on one thing more than any other—your ability to change the behavior and improve the performance of your followers.

The true test of every leader is what their employees do *"in the moment of choice, when nobody is watching."*

Since performance improvement is every leader's greatest challenge and opportunity, the art of R+ behavior change is something every one of us should master.

"My supervisor is the CEO around here."

Unfair as it may be, most of what happens on a day-to-day basis for the average employee is dictated not by the CEO or the board of directors, but by the individual employee's supervisor or manager. When you quit your job, you leave your manager, not your company. Of course, the CEO and senior leadership are involved in enterprise decisions about downsizing, mergers, and the like, but for the most part, it's the frontline supervisor who sets the tone for the employee's perception of the company. And often that perception isn't very pretty.

Remember the story about the lawyer who quit her job to become a waitress? Her boss was always pointing to her mistakes but never complimenting her extra efforts. It was the boss, not the company that caused her to walk away.

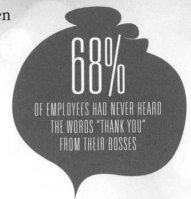

68%
OF EMPLOYEES HAD NEVER HEARD THE WORDS "THANK YOU" FROM THEIR BOSSES

Ken Blanchard coined the term, "Leave Alone/Zap" for this management style. This may help explain why Bob Nelson's research showed that 68 percent of employees had never heard the words "Thank you" from their bosses, even though they consistently rank the need for positive feedback as #1 or #2 in job satisfaction.

We all instinctively know that we feel good when we are given sincere, specific, positive feedback. Why then, are fewer than 30 percent of our leaders using it?

Would your company be happy producing a product that worked properly only 30 percent of the time? Why are we willing to tolerate a management system that manages people properly only 30 percent of the time? The sad truth is that without even knowing it, the majority of leaders today are using Leave Alone/Zap management tactics.

"Feel-Good" Recognition

Christy works for a medical-equipment repair company. Its nearly 700 employees are scattered across the United States, usually with three-to-five per location. They service medical equipment when it breaks.

"I've just taken over HR, and I'm reviewing our corporate recognition program," she said. "I thought we had an effective system until I surveyed our employees and found that 60 percent of them feel our recognition process is useless."

She explained that the company had seven core values that it was trying to recognize. These were the usual qualities you see represented on those posters bearing pictures of waterfalls and mountains: integrity, dedication, teamwork, persistence, and the like.

Christy's company used a Web system that enabled it to single out a core value a particular employee had exemplified. For instance, when an employee demonstrated teamwork, a recommendation went out that the individual be rewarded. The communication would explain what the employee had done to exemplify that core value. The manager could approve or deny the recommendation. If it was approved, the employee would get a gift card or some similar tangible award. Approval was neither immediate nor certain.

Christy continued, "Our problem is that we have a couple of managers who use the system (and perhaps abuse it), and the others don't use it at all. Peer-to-peer participation isn't what we'd like it to be."

"Can you share with me a real-life example of an employee who was recognized and what the employee did to receive this praise?" I asked her.

"Well, it's a bit hard to piece together, since most of our nominations are vague and non-specific," Christy replied. "But we did have one employee who was asked to repair a vital piece of medical equipment which had failed while the patient was on the operating table. It required a part that would not arrive until 24 hours later, and the patient didn't have that long. The employee went to Home Depot and found a part that would work long enough to save the patient. He really saved a life that day."

"That's a great story," I told Christy. "How often does the average employee get a chance to perform an act like that and be recognized for it? Once a month? Once a year?"

We both decided that the average employee would have maybe one chance in a lifetime to qualify for R+ under her current system, which was also plagued by a lack of precision and specificity as to the behaviors that were going to be reinforced.

We helped Christy see that the most important behaviors are the little ones that happen every day. These are the areas to reinforce on a daily basis.

"You're Not Wowing Our Customers!"

Jan, a customer-service manager, quit her job because management wanted her to "wow" her customers, but gave no guidelines on what constituted "wowing."

The CEO informed her that he and the board had listened to recordings of calls between customers and her team of 300 customer-service people. The brass were disappointed in the team's performance. It just wasn't "wowing" the customers.

"I asked him and the board to give me a list of what they wanted me to change in our script to 'wow' our customers," she told me. "That was a year ago and I haven't heard or seen anything since."

No wonder she quit her job as soon as she found a better option.

So What Do You Want Me To Do Exactly?

Since it's so hard for leaders to pinpoint the behaviors that drive improved performance, they often fall into using vague, catch-all terms to describe desired performance. If leaders cannot define the behaviors they need to reinforce, they can hardly expect their followers to do so.

Not Another Baseball Cap

When it comes time to celebrate a success or recognize improvement, you have to figure out what you're going to do. Will it be T-shirts and barbecue this time? Or donuts and coffee? Everyone on the team has a different opinion of what to do. Some will argue for cash, while others sense that cash sends the wrong message. Still others will propose company-logoed baseball caps or coffee mugs.

Many will propose a gift card, and then they will struggle with the handling of the income-tax burden. Will the employee be forced to pay the tax? Or will the company take the huge budget hit of a "payroll gross-up"?

Typically the gift chosen is the one the person with the most political capital likes the best.

Often, we settle on giving them "something with the company logo on it."

This has created an entire industry of companies that warehouse baseball caps, coffee mugs, jackets, pens and the like, all emblazoned with company logos. Now, there's nothing wrong with logo gifts. I have given out thousands of Green Bean pens and other memorabilia as I have spoken around the world, and I've received great feedback.

But the important question is not how the recognition committee feels about logo gifts it chooses. The million-dollar question is, "How do the employees feel about them?" Do they value and appreciate the gifts, and are they using them frequently so that they positively reinforce the desired behaviors? Or do they wind up putting the items on eBay or tossing them in the trash can?

Is the award presented immediately after the behavior occurs, or do we first place the order for shirts, mugs or hats and then hand them out four to six weeks later when everyone has forgotten the milestone we are celebrating?

Many leaders love the idea of their employees marching around with duffle bags and shirts emblazoned with the team logo. *But do these gifts change worker behavior for the better? Do the workers find them to be positive, or punishing?*

Figure 1 offers some interesting insight.

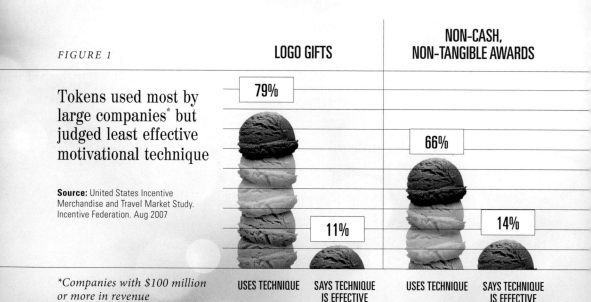

FIGURE 1

LOGO GIFTS

NON-CASH, NON-TANGIBLE AWARDS

Tokens used most by large companies* but judged least effective motivational technique

Source: United States Incentive Merchandise and Travel Market Study. Incentive Federation. Aug 2007

79%

66%

11%

14%

USES TECHNIQUE   SAYS TECHNIQUE IS EFFECTIVE

USES TECHNIQUE   SAYS TECHNIQUE IS EFFECTIVE

*Companies with $100 million or more in revenue

Around the world, I ask my audiences this question, "How many of you have ever received a logoed gift you did not want, need, or use?"

Typically, 98 percent of them raise their hands. And every one of them told the person "thank you" for their gift, which was quickly trashed. I believe we waste a great amount of time and money giving people "stuff" that they don't need or use.

Can logo gifts be effective? Yes, sometimes. But we need to remember that it is the recipient of the gift who decides whether the gift is positive or punishing.

GIFT CARDS FOR MERCHANDISE OR SERVICES		MERCHANDISE		CASH AWARDS	
55%	58%	51%	43%	45%	48%
USES TECHNIQUE	SAYS TECHNIQUE IS EFFECTIVE	USES TECHNIQUE	SAYS TECHNIQUE IS EFFECTIVE	USES TECHNIQUE	SAYS TECHNIQUE IS EFFECTIVE

One company gave out jackets to its workforce, and when it got to the last department, management heard loud complaints from the workers who wanted to know why they were the last to get the jackets.

"You see, they really do like this logo stuff," said the excited plant manager, feeling vindicated in his choice of gifts.

"Well actually, boss," replied his supervisors, "they wanted to put it on eBay and sell it, but since the market is already flooded, they are complaining they can't get anyone to bid on them."

Is it Positive or Punishing?

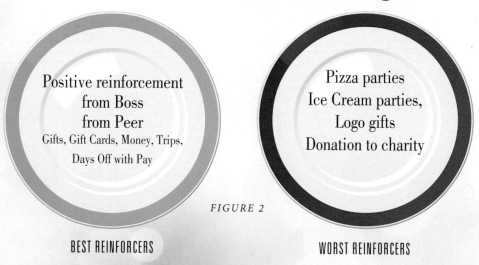

Positive reinforcement
from Boss
from Peer
Gifts, Gift Cards, Money, Trips,
Days Off with Pay

FIGURE 2

Pizza parties
Ice Cream parties,
Logo gifts
Donation to charity

BEST REINFORCERS

WORST REINFORCERS

Ouch.

In surveys of employees, we routinely see logoed gifts ranked as one of the least effective ways to reinforce behavior.

Your Logo Here

"Compensation is a *right*.

Recognition is a *gift*."

– Rosabeth Moss-Kanter

THANK YOU

Isn't a Paycheck Enough?

We hear this quite often from leaders. They spend vast amounts of time and money with consultants to create profit-sharing plans in pursuit of systems that will produce performance improvement. Complex formulas are developed to calculate the payouts, and many employees are clueless about how their system works. While these systems can have impact, they often fail to drive behavior change on a daily basis.

Here are some of the main reasons that these systems fail to produce real behavior change:

- **The positive reinforcement usually comes at the end of the year, or (at most) at the end of the quarter, which isn't often enough to change behavior. Delayed reinforcers fade into the woodwork the minute an *immediate* reinforcer shows up.**

- **The rewards are uncertain, and frequently one person's mistake ruins the payout for everyone.**

- **Pay raises tied to annual performance appraisals are delayed reinforcers. They come just once a year—assuming the appraisals are performed in a timely fashion.**

- **Even worse, the raises are highly subjective or uncertain. Since everyone knows that only a select percentage of employees can be given the highest scores, and thus the best pay raises, the system demotivates and punishes most people.**

Bob Nelson has compiled the following figures:

- *The typical difference between raises for outstanding employees and those for average employees is 3 percent of base salary.*
- *Of the workers surveyed, 81 percent said they would receive no reward for productivity increases.*
- *Of the managers surveyed, 60 percent felt their salaries would not increase should their performances improve.*

"Positive reinforcement? Yeah we get that every Friday, Bill."

The chuckles went up from around the meeting room in Anchorage, Alaska, when a supervisor made that comment after the company vice president had introduced me. I was there conducting a workshop on positive reinforcement with about 150 leaders of a large company.

I got a laugh out of it too. Then I asked the audience how many of them agreed that a paycheck was positive reinforcement.

About half of the people said "no" and the others said "yes," or were noncommittal.

"In case you guys haven't noticed it, you don't agree about this," I told them. "And if you can't agree as to whether something as simple as a paycheck is positive reinforcement, how can your team execute on delivering it consistently?"

The laughter was replaced by silence. Nodding heads told me I had made my point.

"Now, I will answer my own question," I continued.

"A paycheck IS positive reinforcement. It reinforces one behavior, and one behavior alone—the behavior of coming to work. If anyone doesn't believe me, I have a little experiment we can conduct. Just give me your paycheck for the next few weeks, and let's see how long you keep showing up for work."

More laughter.

"So, now that we are clear that a paycheck is R+ for coming to work, let me ask you a question. After the paycheck gets me to work, does it also make me perform my work safely? Does it guarantee that I'll give great customer service, quality or productivity? The answer is no. That is why it takes additional R+ from you leaders to ensure that people perform at their best. My fondest dream is that I will never ever hear another leader say, 'But that's what they are being paid to do.'"

16

I Hate My Boss!

When we talk about positive reinforcement, most people instantly assume that we are talking about managers saying "Good job" and "Thank you." Nothing could be further from the truth.

While these approaches can be positively reinforcing, they can also be punishing. In Saudi Arabia, a young man in one of my classes related that he worked on a project, but knew he had not put the effort into it that he could have. After he delivered his report, his boss told him, "Good job."

The young man said that he was now even more demotivated. He knew his work was substandard, and to have his boss tell him it was "good" made it clear that his boss was either uninterested in his performance, gullible, or simply patronizing him until he could be replaced.

The boss's "Good job" was probably well intended; however the worker found it to be punishing.

A young woman once told me how she felt about "Good job" and "Attagirl!"

"I hate my boss," she lamented. "Every morning I get a text from him that says, 'You're the best' or 'Keep up the good work!'"

"Sounds like a pretty good boss to me," I offered.

"Yes, but I checked with the other girls on my sales team. They get the same text at the exact same time I do."

What could have been R+ had turned to punishment. You can't fake sincerity. And without sincerity, you can't deliver R+.

Positive reinforcement occurs in many forms. But only the recipient can tell us whether what we say or do is really positive or punishing.

17

Chocolate, Vanilla, or Strawberry?
The Great Debate

The most powerful source of motivation is a subject of endless debate. Whether it's Oprah Winfrey, Daniel Pink, or Alfie Kohn, the controversy about what motivates human performance rages on.

Many will argue that rewarding good performance is wrong. They suggest that even a soccer mom jumping up and down and screaming with glee when her five-year-old scores a point is robbing that child of the motivation to play the game.

Hmmm …

To clear up the muddy water, I offer you the following simple model:

All kinds of R+ fall into three categories. I like to think of them as ice cream cones—vanilla, strawberry, and chocolate. (By now, you've probably figured out that I like ice cream.)

The three flavors of R+ are…

Each of these has its relative strengths and weaknesses, and they all play powerful roles in human motivation. Understanding and embracing all of them is the path to performance improvement.

Tangible R+

When you applied for your current job, what was the first question you asked your potential employer? You probably asked what the paycheck was going to be. After that, you asked about benefits, vacation days, sick days, and the like. *Tangible reinforcers form a critical first-level "foundation" that needs to be in place if the other kinds of R+ are to be developed.* There are many forms of tangible R+, and each of these appeal to people in varying degrees. Some examples are cash awards, paychecks, stock options, trips, gifts, logo gifts, gift cards, and time off from work with pay. While many would say that cash is king of all tangible R+, the research proves otherwise. As we pointed out earlier, a paycheck is R+ for one behavior primarily: showing up for work. Once you are at work, the paycheck has done its job. It takes other kinds of R+ to get the performance lift we desire.

cash awards   gift cards   stock options   trips   time off from work with pay

EXAMPLES OF TANGIBLE R+

All too often, companies set up payment systems that are "one-size-fits-all." These systems reward people with more pay regardless of whether they produce any real value to the organization. Google's across-the-board 10 percent pay raise is a glaring and expensive example of this approach. It will undoubtedly foster "entitlement mentality" and an expectation of easy-to-get bonuses in the future.

Social R+

Once a person is coming to work consistently to earn a paycheck, we can add additional reinforcers to boost performance. These can be in the form of additional tangible R+ such as gifts, gift cards, and bonus pay. We can also introduce the idea of social reinforcers.

There are many kinds of social reinforcers. Some of them are positive. And some of them are punishing.

Employee-of-the-Month programs are punishing for most people. Here are some ways you can provide social reinforcers that are positive or rewarding:

- *Ask individual employees for input and listen actively to their responses.*
- *Empower someone to fix a problem.*
- *Give specific, positive, verbal feedback on what a person did correctly.*
- *Allow freedom to work from home (assuming home is a happy place).*
- *And there are more.*

Bob Nelson wrote a whole book on low-cost forms of social R+. Delivering social R+ is both an art and a science. Done well, it can touch someone's heart. Done poorly, it will burn the relationship forever (see Chapter 16, "I Hate My Boss.")

THE CATCH:

The Achilles heel of social R+ is this: You can't positively reinforce some-one who hates your guts. I remember one supervisor who was like Terry Tate, the villain of the Reebok Super Bowl commercial (see Chapter 4: Does Punishment Really Work?). The supervisor was a true punisher of his people. Faced with a unionization attempt, the management team suddenly "got R+ religion" and decided to have an Employee Appreciation Day, with steak dinners for all employees and their families. Even though the "Terry Tate" supervisor was despised by his people, he was placed in charge of grilling the steaks. As the individual workers came up to him with their plates already heavily laden, he put a steak on each plate. One by one, the employees dumped their plates on the supervisor's shoes. They knew he wasn't sincere, and they resented his attempts at manipulating their behavior. The union campaign was successful.

You can't positively reinforce someone who hates your guts.

Self R+

Self-reinforcement is a powerful force. Beholding it at work is awe-inspiring. Operating under self-R+, we humans are at our best. We are the firefighter running into the Twin Towers on 9/11, or perhaps the soldier who jumps on top of the grenade to save his comrades. In such cases of courage and heroism, human beings facing almost certain, immediate, and negative consequences are driven by a much stronger self-reinforcer—the internal reinforcement of sacrifice for another. Self-reinforcement develops over time, as people consistently receive adequate amounts of both tangible and social R+.

THE CATCH

As we pointed out earlier in the story about Leo Inghilleri (Chapter 9: Who Killed the Work Ethic?), some people are very highly self-motivated around work. Others are far more passionate about hunting, fishing, motorcycle riding, knitting, painting, gardening—you name it. We haven't yet invented a way to measure reliably who is and who isn't self-reinforced today at work. Self-reinforcement, by its very definition, is something that you can do only for yourself. Many of the great self-help speakers, such as Anthony Robbins and Brian Tracy, focus on this area.

Maslow's Hierarchy

Maslow's hierarchy of needs, illustrated in Figure 3, actually points to the existence and role of the three flavors of R+. His theory says that the first things people need are the basics: food, money, shelter, clothing—all are forms of tangible R+.

Once these needs are met, we are then looking for social reinforcers, such as positive reinforcement from peers, managers, families, and friends—social R+.

FIGURE 3

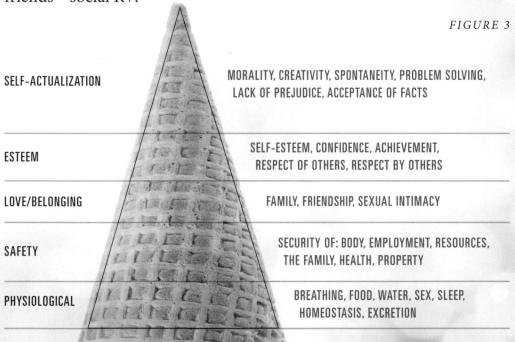

SELF-ACTUALIZATION	MORALITY, CREATIVITY, SPONTANEITY, PROBLEM SOLVING, LACK OF PREJUDICE, ACCEPTANCE OF FACTS
ESTEEM	SELF-ESTEEM, CONFIDENCE, ACHIEVEMENT, RESPECT OF OTHERS, RESPECT BY OTHERS
LOVE/BELONGING	FAMILY, FRIENDSHIP, SEXUAL INTIMACY
SAFETY	SECURITY OF: BODY, EMPLOYMENT, RESOURCES, THE FAMILY, HEALTH, PROPERTY
PHYSIOLOGICAL	BREATHING, FOOD, WATER, SEX, SLEEP, HOMEOSTASIS, EXCRETION

Once all of these needs are met we are looking to "self-actualize"—to engage in things that allow us to reinforce ourselves positively. A wise man once said that it is better to give than to receive. Whether it's the billionaire donating his fortune to help fight cancer, or a volunteer in the hospital who helps a family deal with grief, what you are seeing is people engaging in behavior that produces some level of internal or self-reinforcement—self-R+.

The Reinforcement Continuum model (Figure 4) helps us to see how we respond to the three kinds of R+.

FIGURE 4

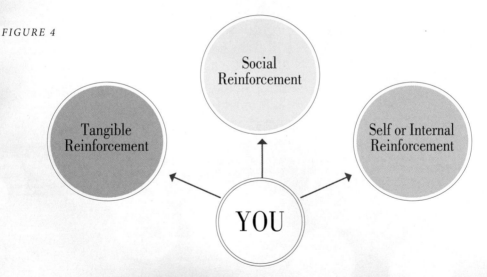

The Reinforcement Continuum
The types of reinforcement that motivate you most powerfully today will change tomorrow and they will quite often not motivate me or the next person.

When we first go to work at a new job, we are primarily engaging in that behavior to get a paycheck; so tangible R+ is the most important. Over time, as we get to know our coworkers and managers, and as we develop relationships and trust, they will be able to influence our behavior positively using social reinforcers. Eventually, we develop self-reinforcers for ourselves to continue in the desired habits.

Getting an employee to this level is a slow process, and quite often someone steps in to derail it. Suppose a worker is behaving and performing at the highest level. Then the company announces downsizing, pay cuts, and more work to be done by fewer people.

Yep, the process just got derailed. The worker will slide down the scale of cynicism, performing just well enough to get a paycheck. As soon as another job offer opens up, the employee is lost, gone to another employer.

All of the Above

So which kind of R+ is best? All of them are. It depends on the performer. Can we get behavior change by using only social R+? Sure we can. You can get to Alaska from Florida on a bicycle if you are determined enough and patient enough. But you can get there a lot faster if you hop on a plane.

I'm not in business to get performance improvement and behavior change slowly. I'm interested in getting it faster than my competitors, and sustaining it better than they can. If you feel the same way, be sure you embrace all three flavors of R+ in your leadership systems.

18

Empowering Employees Is R∗

Command & Control is Punishing

During the 1960s and 1970s, American textile companies were being squeezed in the death grip of cheaper offshore labor. One by one, in small towns all over the Southeast, the factories were shuttered and closed. Places such as Sylacauga, Alabama, and Lancaster, South Carolina, became ghost towns, as production was moved to South and Central America. This decline was the beginning of a larger erosion of American manufacturing capacity, with a huge loss of jobs and a negative impact on the U.S. economy.

While the war against cheap overseas labor was eventually lost, some incredible battles were won along the way.

One winner was Riegel Textile's CEO, Bob Coleman. Unlike many of his "command-and-control" old-school peers, Bob learned to tap the innovation and creativity of his people, achieving amazing results. He was an early pioneer of the Zero Defects concept, wherein a team of employees, called an "advisory board," identified opportunities to improve quality, efficiency and safety. These Zero Defects teams were the forerunners of quality circles and the "lean manufacturing" movements of today.

Bob subscribed to the theory that nobody knows the job better than the person who does it eight hours a day.

Using his Zero Defects secret weapon, Bob was able to purchase a textile mill and take it from 72 percent efficiency to 96 percent.

Why does empowering people to change their surroundings have such a huge impact? Research shows that one of the key drivers of employee satisfaction (read R+) is "being able to make a difference at work." Giving people the autonomy to change the process to remove negative and punishing consequences, is a huge, untapped source of positive reinforcement.

In his book, *It's Your Ship*, Michael D. Abrashoff discovered the same lessons learned by Coleman. Rising out of the Navy's bureaucracy, he was finally given command of the destroyer, *Benfold*, in the Pacific Fleet. During

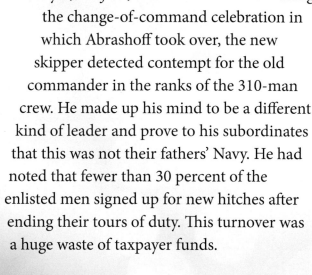

the change-of-command celebration in which Abrashoff took over, the new skipper detected contempt for the old commander in the ranks of the 310-man crew. He made up his mind to be a different kind of leader and prove to his subordinates that this was not their fathers' Navy. He had noted that fewer than 30 percent of the enlisted men signed up for new hitches after ending their tours of duty. This turnover was a huge waste of taxpayer funds.

Early on, he scheduled interviews with five crew members every day, taking notes:

> **"Why did you join the Navy?"**
> **"Are you married?"**
> **"Tell me about your kids."**
> **"What are we doing here that we could do better?"**
> **"Why do we do things the way we do them?"**
> **"Is there a better way?"**

Not only did he spend a lot of time asking people for their ideas; he also communicated his own thoughts to his crew, using the ship's PA system. Silence breeds mistrust of leadership, he reasoned. In fact, he communicated so much and so well that his crew nicknamed him, "Mega Mike."

Periodically, to break up the monotony of shipboard life, the crew organized a grill-out party at the stern of the ship. Under the old commander, enlisted men had been required to go through the food line only after the officers had filled their plates and retired to their special mess hall.

One day without saying a word, Commander Abrashoff went to the back of the line, while the rest of his officers were at the front. They motioned for him to come up front, but he declined. If the food ran out, he said, he would go without. Next, he began eating with the enlisted men, instead of with the officers, asking questions and learning all the time.

Before long, guess what? The other officers began following his example, bringing about a huge culture change and eliminating the class society that had been established.

Did listening to people pay off? You bet it did.

Under Michael's command, the *Benfold* went from 30 percent staff retention to 100 percent. It became the "go-to" ship in the Navy, with unprecedented accuracy and reliability. The crew was allowed to implement radical new ideas that greatly improved efficiency and reliability.

The lesson is clear.

The truly powerful leaders are those with the confidence to delegate power to those who are beneath them. They are confident their people will follow them whether they are standing there or not.

19

What Makes A Great Leader?

Take a minute before turning this page, and write down 10 core traits of great leaders. (No peeking on the next page)

1.

2.

3.

4.

5.

6.

7.

8.

9.

10.

In the leadership courses I teach, here are the traits most commonly listed:

Good communication skills
Trustworthiness
Willingness to listen
Knowledge and experience
Good attitude
Accountability
Ability to motivate
Integrity
Courage
Ability to stay organized
Ability to inspire respect

How do they match your list?

My point is this: Almost everyone agrees on what good leaders must do, and how they must act.

In fact, here is what some of the greatest leaders have said:

"There are two things people want more than money: recognition and praise."
—Mary Kay Ash

"Trust, not technology, is the issue of the decade."
—Tom Peters

"Nobody cares how much you know until they know how much you care."
— John Wooden,
UCLA basketball coach

But there is one quality of leaders that trumps all the others, and it is the one that nobody guesses.

To help you identify it, fill in the blanks here:

> **If every employee gave us perfect human performance, we wouldn't need** _____
>
> **The measure of a Leader is what the followers do in the moment of** _____ **when nobody is** _____ **. The most important ability of leaders is the** _____ **to change the** _____ **of their followers.**

See the answers below.

To help you identify the leadership quality that trumps all others, see the completed sentences below:

If every employee gave us perfect human performance, we wouldn't need managers. The measure of a leader is what the followers do in the moment of choice when nobody is watching. The most important ability of leaders is the ability to change the behavior of their followers.

So as a leader, only one thing really matters—what your people do when you leave. This quality may be defined as "leadership that sticks."

That and that alone defines your ability to deliver and sustain R+ to drive high performance.

As the graphic below illustrates, ***employee engagement drives the engine of business success.*** And R+ drives employee engagement. In short, R+ is the fuel you put in the tank of your corporate culture.

FIGURE 5

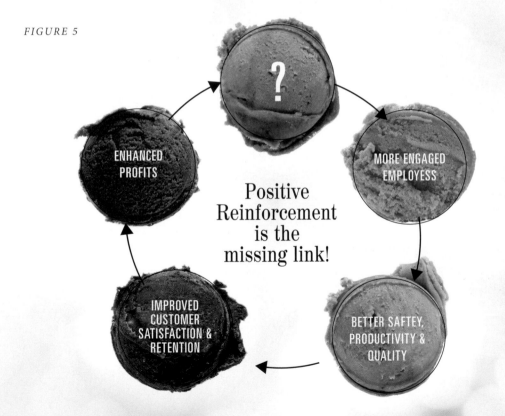

Positive Reinforcement is the missing link!

ENHANCED PROFITS

?

MORE ENGAGED EMPLOYESS

BETTER SAFTEY, PRODUCTIVITY & QUALITY

IMPROVED CUSTOMER SATISFACTION & RETENTION

But instead of providing the reinforcers that drive great performance, most managers use **LEAVE ALONE/ZAP**. What is that?

Wayne, who works for one of the largest retailers in the United States, tells this story:

> *I helped a woman the other day in the Garden section. Later, I found out that she was so impressed with my help and service that she went to my manager and told him that she would only be coming to our store from now on, even though it wasn't the one closest to her house. I never got any recognition for that, not even a "Good job." It's not like I expected a raise; just a "Thank you." What kind of incentive do I have to go "Above and Beyond" if I can't even be appreciated or acknowledged when I do?*

Figure 6 depicts the various "buckets" that your employees fit into. Let's hope your training systems are effective, so that people are clear on their mission and are equipped with the tools and skills they need to do the job. Assuming you have done your homework here, then none of your people fall into the first bucket, "I can't do it." That leaves three buckets remaining: Non-compliant, Compliant, and Committed.

FIGURE 6

Types of Employee Behavior

Where do you want your culture?

The answer is obvious: You want commitment. You want people who deliver safety, quality, production, and client satisfaction "in the moment of choice, when no one is watching."

But, how do you move people from non-compliance to commitment?

The sad truth is that most of our managers use the tool we all learned from the police: Leave Alone/Zap.

Leave Alone/Zap does produce a behavior change—at least temporarily. You can see it while you're riding down the Interstate. If you're like me, you and everyone else are driving 10 miles per hour over the speed limit. Guess what? That makes you non-compliant, as Figure 7 shows.

FIGURE 7

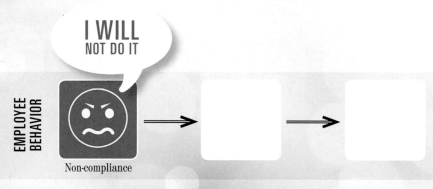

This continues until you see a police officer pointing a radar gun at you. To avoid the "Zap!" what do you do?

You hit the brakes. And so now, to avoid the Zap! you are Compliant (Figure 8).

FIGURE 8

This newfound change you have adopted is short-lived however. About 60 seconds after you pass the cop you breathe a sigh of relief—"Whew! He didn't get me"—and then what do you do?

You hit the gas. Once again, you are non-compliant. The same scenario plays out billions of time a day:

The students in a noisy classroom misbehave until the teacher enters the room.

A group of employees slacks off and chit chats until someone tips them off that the boss is coming.

The point is that Leave Alone/Zap fails to produce behavior change in the "moment of choice, when nobody is watching." It doesn't get you commitment; nor does it get you employee engagement.

The Power of R+

But positive reinforcement does lead to that commitment, and a whole lot more.

FIGURE 9

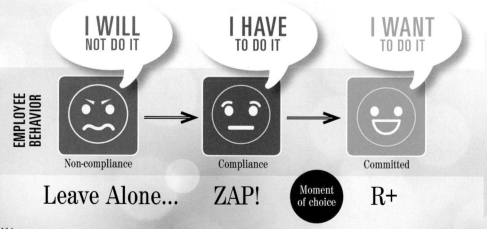

So how well does your management system do at delivering the positive reinforcement people need and crave?

By now you may be getting the picture that your management system has more than its fair share of Leave Alone/Zap.

You are probably thinking that you'd like more positive reinforcement in your culture…and a whole lot less Leave Alone/Zap!

But how do you get from where you are to where you want to be?

That is the million-dollar question. And I'm going to answer that for you.

In your journey, where is your culture? You have only two choices: Company A or Company B. Which company sounds like yours?

Company A:

"To be honest, when it comes to positive reinforcement, we pretty much rely on MAGIC. When we get it right, it's kind of like pulling the R+ rabbit out of the hat. We're amazed at the results. But it's pretty much a hit-and-miss thing around here. We have an inconsistent definition of what positive reinforcement is. We have our fair share of "Leave Alone/Zap" managers, and we have no real way to measure how well we are doing at delivering R+ to our team."

Or...

Company B :

"I'd say that we are STRATEGIC with R+. We have a clear and consistent definition of what positive reinforcement is, and we execute daily on a strategy of delivering it—from the CEO to the mail room. Here's the report to prove it."

It really doesn't matter where you are on the (Positive Reinforcement) PR+ Spectrum. The only thing that matters is where you want to be. And that is as far toward the Company B model as you can go.

Watch the "All Over It" video by visiting
www.powerofpositivereinforcement.com

20

Why Green Beans & Ice Cream?

The lesson Mom taught me about green beans and ice cream ranks with the most important lessons I've learned in life. Mom figured out what she needed from me, and in her own very special way she got me to want to do it.

You can put Mom's system to work in your team.

First, you have to pinpoint the behaviors you want, and positively reinforce them immediately when you see them.

Decide what you want people to do. Focus on the behaviors that drive the results you need. Training has a place, but positive reinforcement is the most powerful factor in sustaining high performance. Speed-limit signs, by themselves do not stop speeders. But consequences do. Positive consequences are always better than punishing ones. The trick is to leverage positive consequences to get people where you want them and to put an end to the negative consequences that shut down and stifle your team, preventing it from performing at its best.

As clear as the model in Figure 10 is, few leaders embrace it. Just ask their employees. The vast majority of today's workers (more than 70 percent) will tell you that they have never heard a "Thank you" from their leadership team (supervisors, managers, executives).

FIGURE 10

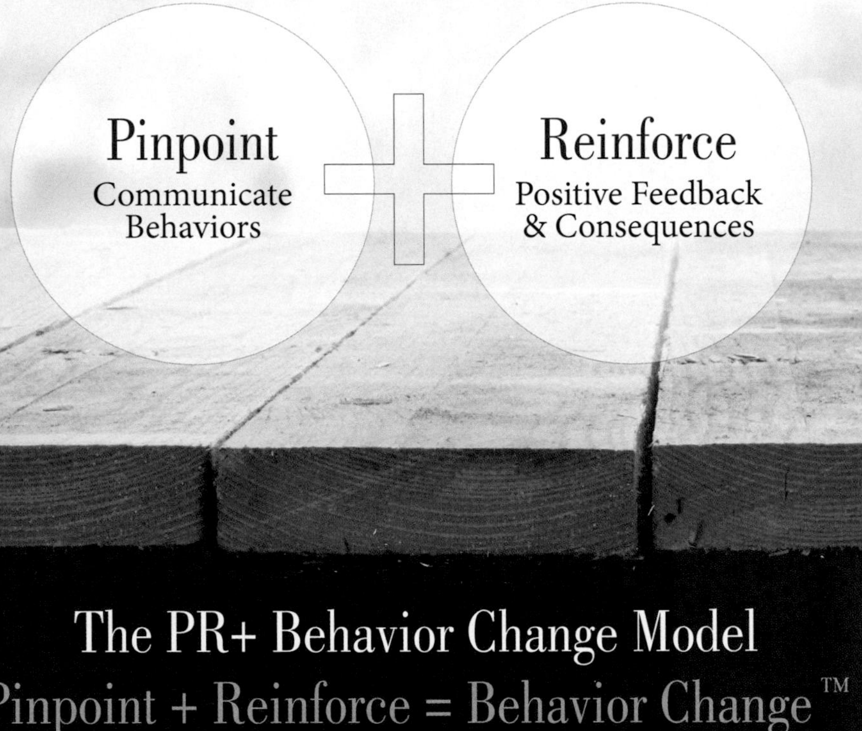

Pinpoint
Communicate
Behaviors

Reinforce
Positive Feedback
& Consequences

The PR+ Behavior Change Model
Pinpoint + Reinforce = Behavior Change ™

Find specific things to reinforce positively every day in the actions of people with whom you live and work. Make sure your positives far outweigh the negatives. Remember you need four positive comments for every one negative comment—just to stay even. This doesn't imply that you have to find something negative to say, but that if you do have to correct or even punish, at least four positive comments are necessary to maintain positive performance change.

The book *Chicken Soup for the Soul* by Jack Canfield and Mark Victor Hansen contains a touching story about positive reinforcement that saved the life of a suicidal teenager.

I would like to share that story with you at www.powerofpositivereinforcement.com

Yes, that day with Mom and Green Beans & Ice Cream changed my life forever. I know that as you focus on giving positive reinforcement to your family, friends, coworkers and yourself every day, you will be amazed at the results.

What now?

I hope you enjoyed reading this, my very first book, as much as I enjoyed writing it! But this is only the tip of the iceberg…there is so much more to learn!

I cover some of this in the final video at the link below. I hope you see the end of this book as the beginning to a new way of life. If you want to learn more about our Power of Positive Reinforcement DVD, webinars, and workshops, as well as our Smartcard Reinforcement System™ please visit us on the web at www.greenbeanleadership.com today!

I have a few closing thoughts in a final video for you at the link below.

 www.powerofpositivereinforcement.com

About The Author

Bill Sims, Jr., is President of The Bill Sims Company, Inc. For nearly 30 years, Bill has created behavior-based recognition programs that have helped large and small firms to deliver positive reinforcement to inspire better performance from employees and increase bottom line profits.

Bill has delivered his "Green Beans & Ice Cream" leadership workshop and keynote speeches in Europe, the Middle East, most of the USA, Australia and many parts of Africa.

This book is based on these sessions and his experience having built more than 1,000 positive reinforcement systems programs at firms including DuPont, Siemens VDO, Coca-Cola, and Disney, to name a few.

To learn more visit us at www.greenbeanleadership.com today.

PR+ leadership...One Scoop At a Time

I'm delighted that you have taken the time to explore my ideas in positive reinforcement and behavior change!

I hope that this small keepsake will help you remember the power of positive reinforcement. Before you know it, you will be dishing out scoops of positive feedback to others every single day. You see, this little tool is not only cute, it is powerful. It will help you change yourself, and master the power of positive reinforcement.

Start every day with all the ice cream cones lying on your desk, or in your pocket. Make it a goal to say something positive to at least three people every day (your kids, your spouse, your boss, your coworkers, and yes, even yourself!). Tell them what they did, and why that mattered to you. It's that simple.

Why not start right now with someone who made a difference to you?

Every time you positively reinforce someone, reward yourself and put one ice cream cone in the base. Don't go to bed until all three cones are back in their place.

Have fun!

Got a story about how Green Beans & Ice Cream made a difference in your life? Want to order a copy of our free DVD for your leadership team? Visit us at www.behaviorchangenow.com today!

Order your Green Beans Keepsake at www.threescoopsaday.com

WHAT OTHERS ARE SAYING...

We purchased a Simple Truths' gift book for our conference in Lisbon, Spain. We also personalized it with a note on the first page about valuing innovation. I've never had such positive feedback on any gift we've given. People just keep talking about how much they valued the book and how perfectly it tied back to our conference message.

— **Michael R. Marcey,** Efficient Capital Management, LLC.

The small inspirational books by Simple Truths are amazing magic! They spark my spirit and energize my soul.

— **Jeff Hughes,** United Airlines

Mr. Anderson, ever since a friend of mine sent me the 212° movie online, I have become a raving fan of Simple Truths. I love and appreciate the positive messages your products convey and I have found many ways to use them. Thank you for your vision.

— **Patrick Shaughnessy,** AVI Communications, Inc.

If you have enjoyed this book we invite you to check out our entire collection of gift books, with free inspirational movies, at www.simpletruths.com. You'll discover it's a great way to inspire friends and family, or to thank your best customers and employees.

The simple truths®
Difference

Catch the Wind

Catch the Wind

A BOOK OF WINDMILLS AND WINDPOWER

written by Landt Dennis

photographs by Lisl Dennis

FOUR WINDS PRESS   NEW YORK

LIBRARY OF CONGRESS CATALOGING IN PUBLICATION DATA

Dennis, Landt.
    Catch the wind.

    Bibliography: p.
    Includes index.
    1. Windmills—History—Juvenile literature.   2. Wind
power—History—Juvenile literature.   I. Dennis, Lisl.
II. Title.
TJ823.D39   621.4'5'09   75–45002
ISBN 0–590–07414–8

Published by Four Winds Press

A Division of Scholastic Magazines, Inc., New York, N.Y.

Text copyright © 1976 by Landt Dennis

Photographs copyright © 1976 by Lisl Dennis

All rights reserved

Printed in the United States of America

Library of Congress Catalog Card Number: 75–45002

5 4 3   80 79 78

Acknowledgments

The author and photographer wish to express their gratitude to the following researchers and proponents of windpower. Without their cooperation and enthusiasm, this book would not have been possible.

Cees Van Hees
Piet Myksenaar
Arie Butterman
Melleken Muysken
Jacob Kaal
Arie Berkhout
William E. Heronemus
Tom Chalk
Thomas E. Sweeney
R. Buckminster Fuller
Neil and Polly Welliver
Henry Clews
Margaretha de Meyere
Stewart Udall
Hank Fisher
Jack and Jessica Dickson
P.H. van Malsen
Johan Jansen
Hans Meyer

Contents

Catch the Wind

1
Why Windpower?

An eighteenth-century European windmill of unusual design.

Leaves blow. Papers scatter. Kites fly. These are a few of the countless results of a natural phenomenon which, until recently, most people took for granted and only a handful of scientists paid much attention to—the wind.

In the current search for alternate energy sources, however, the practicality of windpower is being considered more seriously than ever before. Nations of the world are finally coming to realize that fossil fuel —oil, coal and natural gas formed beneath the earth from plant life buried there for millions of years— does not exist in infinite supplies. In fact, many scientists tell us that if the world continues at its current rate of per capita energy consumption, we could exhaust fossil-fuel supplies by the year 2000.

Because of the limited supplies of fossil fuel available, the price the consumer pays continues to mount. Heating bills for homes, gasoline costs for cars, electricity charges for lights, appliances, and television sets are all going to take a larger portion of the wage earner's salary.

A further problem with the world's dependence on fossil fuel is that it pours out waste heat, as well as contributes to the pollution of our air. Today, in fact, there is an often-visible layer of pollution which covers heavily populated or industrialized areas of the world. Acting as a blanket over the atmosphere, it traps solar radiation and prevents its escape.

The danger is that the most minute change in the world's overall temperature could melt the antarctic ice cap, which contains over 80 percent of the world's ice, sending forth a flood that would cover the Empire State Building and millions of people along the way. Climatologists say that as a result of the blanket of pollution existing over our earth right now the climate is beginning to change. Glaciers long frozen with age in both Switzerland and Alaska are already beginning to warm up, in fact.[1]

The result of this worldwide energy crisis, which if not solved could completely alter the living style and standards of the world, has been an accelerated search for alternative sources of energy, including coal gasification and geothermal, tidal and hydroelectric power. Electricity from nuclear fission, however, has probably been the most seriously considered solution to mankind's energy needs. Frought with controversy, the few nuclear energy plants in existence are located mainly in Europe. Some nuclear energy plants have even been abandoned because of technical difficulties after millions of dollars went into their construction.

Nuclear energy is produced by splitting uranium atoms and in the process vast amounts of energy are released. However, scientists must contend with the disposal of radioactive wastes that result from the process, and therein lies the controversial aspect of nuclear energy.

The result, according to energy expert Wilson Clark, has caused nuclear fission to be "associated in the public mind with the atomic bomb, and has triggered a debate over public safety unequaled in the development of any technology in human history. Its proponents in industry and government claim that nuclear energy will usher in an unprecedented age of clean and cheap power. Its detractors argue that its development will bring civilization to a grinding halt in the wake of stifling radioactive pollution of the planet."[2]

But the wind is an energy source that is free to all mankind, infinite in supply, and nonpolluting, and it has been throughout history a force which has intrigued thinkers.

What causes wind? First, there is a constant interchange of air between the cold polar caps and the warm tropics. Air becomes compressed when it is cold and expands when it is warmed up. Therefore, the slightest temperature change can cause the movement of great bodies of air. Wind is also produced by the rotation of the earth. At the equator the earth is moving as fast as 1,000 mph and produces a great sea of air around its circumference.

It is these two forces which produce the wind systems, both small and large, which surround our globe.

At times the wind can be gentle as a spring breeze, and at other times as powerful as a cyclone, hurricane, or typhoon. It can bring rain in abundance to places such as the Caribbean, while elsewhere its ab-

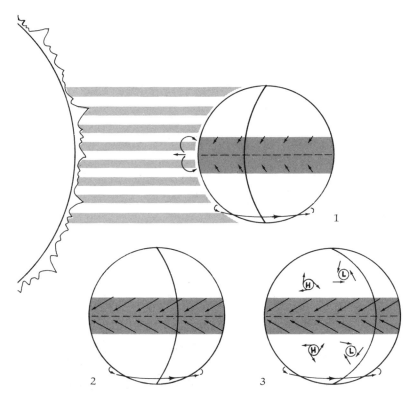

1) Air over the equator gets most heat from the sun. Cool air is constantly moving from both hemispheres toward the equator. 2) But because of the earth's rotation, the cool winds are deflected from east to west, causing prevailing east winds at the equator. 3) In the northern hemisphere, winds flow clockwise round high-pressure areas, and counterclockwise round low-pressure areas; in the southern hemisphere winds blow in the opposite way round highs and lows.

The wind makes clouds billow, paper scatter, windmills turn.
In eighteenth-century Holland, over 9,000 mills once operated.

sence can result in deserts. The warm air and moisture the wind carries from the south keeps northern Europe from being a polar waste, while its gentle breezes help to stifle the heat of South America's tropical west coast.

Windpower has even made a country. Without the wind to power the windmills which pump the water away from its marshes and estuaries, thus creating dry land, Holland might still be a slave to the sea. Instead, with as many as 9,000 windmills at work at one time, she has become an important European nation.

For centuries, navigators were also completely dependent on the wind as a source of energy. The daily ship's log of seagoing captains of the fifteenth, sixteenth, or seventeenth centuries records how the wind was cursed for its absence and idolized when it filled the ships' sails and powered them across the great oceans and seas of the world, making possible exploration of new lands, such as America and Australia. Navigators have, in fact, given names to the established bodies of winds which buffet the earth's surface, often seasonally, sometimes year round. The barber wind, the poison wind, the doctor wind, the wind-of-120-days, the roaring 40s, and the howling 50s are all among the earth's wind systems, as well as Alaska's knik, Japan's narai, and Argentina's pampero.

It is the great wind systems, moreover, that are the major influence on weather. Southern Asia is at the mercy of the monsoons, while northern Europe is warmed by the friendly Gulf Stream whose direction is controlled by the westerlies. And the west coast of South America is teeming with sea nutrients that are brought by the antarctic winds that push the Humboldt Current along its shores.

For early navigators, the strength of these winds could be frightening. The North Atlantic trade winds, blowing west with great constancy from North Africa, were in fact a source of major concern to Columbus's sailors. The men wondered how they would be able to sail back to Spain against these winds. Fortunately, they discovered the westerlies further to the north, which blew the sailors safely back to the court of King Ferdinand and Queen Isabella.

Ferdinand Magellan experienced similar anxiety and relief on his famous round-the-world voyage from 1519 to 1521. All the way across the Atlantic and down the east coast of South America, he and his men were carried along by the gentle trade winds. Nearing Cape Horn and falling below the 40th parallel, they faced a surprise. Here they were introduced to the roaring 40s, a howling, terrifying body of air that whips around the world in an easterly direction and can reach speeds up to 50 knots. Braving the uncertainty of such a formidable encounter, Magellan rounded the cape, where to his joy he found another set of gentle trade winds to carry him across the Pacific.

With time, ships began to follow these great wind routes in the same way that trucks and passenger cars today speed along the world's major highways. One particularly popular windway was from England along the Canary Current to Africa. Ships would set out loaded with cargoes of cloth and beads, which their captains would swap for a hold full of slaves in

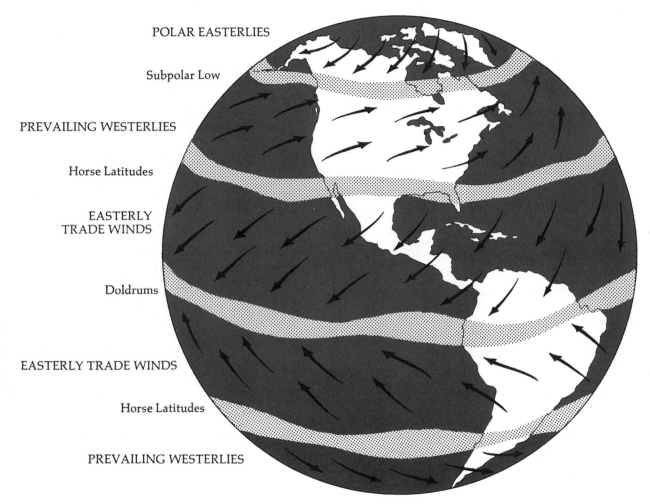

POLAR EASTERLIES

Subpolar Low

PREVAILING WESTERLIES

Horse Latitudes

EASTERLY
TRADE WINDS

Doldrums

EASTERLY TRADE WINDS

Horse Latitudes

PREVAILING WESTERLIES

Subpolar Low and POLAR EASTERLIES (not visible)

This diagram shows the prevailing surface winds that girdle the globe; the arrows indicate the direction in which they blow. In the hot, sticky doldrums near the equator, there is little wind. The air, warmed by the equatorial sun, rises straight up while cooler air from north and south moves in to take its place as the easterly trade winds. With average speeds of 10 to 15 knots, these trade winds are the most constant on the planet. The horse latitudes, or belts of subtropical calm, are zones of downward vertical air movement where warm air earlier forced up from the doldrums returns to the Earth's surface and divides into two streams. One stream moves toward the equator again as part of the easterly trade winds. The other joins the prevailing westerlies as they blow poleward. At the poles, meanwhile (the South Pole is not shown here), cold air in the polar easterlies starts toward the equator. The subpolar lows, where these winds meet, are among the stormiest places on Earth.

Africa. Then they would proceed to the West Indies on the trade winds. From there, loaded with rum and molasses, they would return home on the westerlies. The end result, especially for the captains, was a purse spilling over with profits.

For centuries, however, no serious study was made of the wind. It wasn't until the middle of the nineteenth century that a U.S. Navy hydrographer, Matthew Fontaine Maury, produced a map of the world's winds, pinpointing over 52 systems. Through the meticulous study of thousands of ships' logs, he slowly and accurately pieced together the jigsaw puzzle which told what to expect of the earth's atmosphere in specific parts of the world, on a regular basis. It was Maury's research which showed that a longer sea route between two points can sometimes result in speedier travel. For example, if an English ship headed for Sydney, Australia, filled her sails with trade winds to Brazil, then crossed back to South Africa, it often got the captain and his crew to their destination twice as fast as if they hugged the West African coastline. While they might have saved thousands of travel miles by following the shore route,

Clipper ships, unfurling hundreds of sails, were driven by the wind across the earth's oceans in the eighteenth and nineteenth centuries. Matthew Maury, a navy mapmaker, realized that there were 52 wind "systems," or highways, for captains to follow.

the winds weren't to their advantage and therefore the trip would have taken much longer.

By the middle of the nineteenth century it was learned that daily weather is caused by the movement of zones of high- and low-pressure air. These can extend for hundreds, perhaps thousands, of miles. A good way to understand this is to think of a balloon. Inside the balloon is a high-pressure zone caused by the concentration of a great deal of air in a small area. When an area of high pressure is next to one of low pressure, then the air rushes from the high toward the low. When you release the pressure on the end of a balloon, the air rushes out. This movement of air from high- to low-pressure zones is the underlying law of meteorology, or the science of weather study.

In some areas of the world at certain times during the year, great land masses are regularly affected by a change in air pressure. The monsoons are the result of such a change. In the torrid summers of Asia, the earth heats up. This makes the air light. And since heat rises, the air begins to lift off the earth. Soon, a low-pressure area is formed and to fill it in, air from as far away as Australia rushes in. As it passes over the Indian Ocean and the Pacific, it picks up moisture. Later, it drops it in torrential quantities on the jungles and cities and farmlands of Malaysia, India, and as far north as Japan.

Each June, the monsoons mark the beginning of the planting season. But then in the winter, the great Asian land mass drops its temperature, causing the air overhead to cool off, and a great high-pressure area is formed. This movement of air means snow for the Himalayas. For sea-level lands, it is a time for cloudless skies and brilliant sunshine. Areas that may have had as much as 25 inches of rainfall in June experience no rainfall at all in March.

This change is not nearly as dramatic, however, as what the wind is able to produce in other parts of the world. The chinook is an infamous wind which blows over Montana and Alberta, Canada, and drops rain and snow on the western half of the Rockies. Skiers and farmers profit from this blessing, but once the wind has wrung itself out, it becomes hot and dry. In Harve, Montana, the chinook shot the temperature

up 31 degrees in three minutes. But even more spectacular was its performance in Calgary, Alberta, when one day in February the thermometer hurtled from a low of 14 degrees below zero to a record-breaking 76 degrees above.

Most of the time, though, the wind's peculiarities do no harm. But at other times, its destructive power is enormous. Iran's wind-of-120-days carries with it so much force and sand that it has been known to bury entire villages. And in southern California, the Santa Ana wind triggers raging brush fires. A norther pulling in cold arctic air can wreak havoc with the Florida citrus crop. Millions of dollars of fruit can be wiped out overnight as temperatures plummet from 80 to 25 degrees.

The Italians, Spaniards, and Frenchmen all curse the sirocco wind, which sweeps over the Sahara Desert and gathers up moisture over the Mediter-

Daumier, the nineteenth-century French artist, knew the power of the wind. Often gentle as a lamb, it has been recorded at 231 mph at Mt. Washington, N.H. Once harnessed, wind is a source of energy.

ranean, bringing stultifying humidity to western Europe. Judges have even been known to be more lenient in passing sentences for offenses committed during a sirocco.

Another treacherous wind, known in France as the mistral, has been known to overturn trucks and blow railroad cars into the air like so many match sticks.

Gentle as a lamb at times, powerful as a giant at others, awkward or amazingly civilized at others, the wind has been harnessed by man most frequently through the erection of windmills.

In his attempts to harness the wind, man has relied on the windmill for thousands of years. Based on the simplest of principles, sails or blades, turned by the wind like a pinwheel, are attached to a shaft. The resistance of the sails to the wind causes the shaft to rotate and, either directly or via a series of gears and couplings, activates the millstone, pump, electric generator, or some other machinery, depending on the size, design, and intended purpose of the windmill.

Such a seemingly old-fashioned device may seem foolish and outdated to some. But when you compare the wind's infinite availability to the present dwindling supply of fossil fuel, a reevaluation of this energy source whose origin dates back to the seventeenth century B.C. seems necessary.

2
The Early History of Windmills

The earliest known record of man's use of windpower is from the twentieth century B.C., when the Babylonian Emperor Hammurabi planned to use windmills for irrigation. Later, in the second century B.C., Hero of Alexandria described a windmill in his writings. Remarkably enough, this one was used to play an organ.

Since early man was dependent on himself or his oxen to grind his grain between two millstones or to lift water from a stream to fill his irrigation ditches, the discovery of windpower must have caused much rejoicing. Here was a way to ease the struggle for survival by increasing the yield of the land, turning the harvest more quickly into bread, and at the same time decreasing the amount of manpower needed to do it.

History reveals that it was the Europeans who took greatest advantage of the windmill and developed its design to the size and variety of usefulness best typified by those found in Holland.

This nineteenth-century U.S. mill hoisted goods to a loft.

The earliest record of man's use of windpower dates from the twentieth century B.C. Babylonian Emperor Hammurabi used windmills for irrigation. This second-century B.C. windmill was different, though. Hero of Alexandria used it to pump an organ's piston.

But how did the idea of windmills reach Europe from its birthplace thousands of miles away? It has been suggested by historians that traders at the time of Jesus, passing through Seistan, on the present Iranian-Afghanistanian border, saw wind machines being used to grind grain and brought the concept back to northern Europe. The discovery in Holland's Friesland of a thousand silver coins used in India three hundred years before the Crusades adds more credibility to the theory, and proves that trade between the two areas was prevalent at that time.

By the year 1000 A.D., however, theory vanishes and established fact begins. Records show that windmills were definitely in operation in Europe by then. It is recorded that in 1105 a French convent built both a water mill and a windmill. But the earliest illustration to accompany a written record of a windmill is in the Windmill Psalter, an English manuscript of 1270 believed to have been created at Canterbury. Other early depictions of windmills include a memorial brass in the English seaport town of King Lynne, which commemorates the mayor, Adam de

The first windmill used in the Middle East had a vertical axis. Later models, such as this one, were developed for use in Europe in the late sixteenth century.

Walsoken, who died of the Black Death in 1348, and a picture of a windmill in a French illustrated manuscript of 1420.

But a difficult question arose at the end of the fourteenth century in Europe: Was the air used by the windmills owned by the church or by the landowner? Tithing, the giving of 10 percent of one's earnings to the church, was accepted at the time, but to assure an even greater income Pope Celestine III laid claim to the air. Windmills could use his air, he said, but at a price.

A fascinating dispute at the end of the fourteenth century reinforced the ruling in favor of the church. The Augustine monks of the Abbey at Windsheim in Holland wanted to build a windmill near Zwoll. But the neighboring lord claimed that the wind in the entire district was his. Thereupon the monks took their case to the Bishop of Utrecht, under whose jurisdiction the province had been since the tenth century, and the bishop insisted that the wind belonged to him, not to the lord.

One landowner, Dean Herbert, tried to get away

with building a windmill without the church's consent. Jocelin's Chronicle, written from 1173 to 1202, tells of his attempt. "I tell thee, it will not be without damage to my own mill," the Abbott, concerned about the competition, wrote Herbert. "The townfolk will go to thy mill, and grind their corn at their own pleasure; nor can I hinder them, since they are free men. I will allow no new mill on such principle." Troops were sent to dismantle Herbert's mill, but when they arrived, it was gone. Herbert had cleverly run off with it in order to save the valuable wood.

Other chronicles reveal similar mysterious disappearances when it came time for the farmer to collect his ground grain. Somehow, it seemed, a portion of the grain always got siphoned off into the miller's own bag. In fact, the percentage that an English miller was legitimately justified in keeping as payment for his labor was known as the "knaveship," hardly a term to convey anything short of outright roguery.

Finally the law stepped in to set up definite rules by which the miller would be paid, but they were so

This windmill, with a horizontal axis, was invented in the twelfth century in the North Sea area of Europe. It is a tower mill. Only the top turns in the wind.

complicated that, in 1769, payment in money became compulsory. Since this law did not entirely prevent millers from cheating their customers, an additional law passed in the eighteenth century required that "every miller shall put up in his mill a table of prices for grinding or the amount of toll required at his mill, under a penalty not exceeding 20s. All penalties to go half to the informer and the other half to the poor."[3] This new law, it was hoped, would eliminate the problem of theft at last. Continued complaints show, however, that millers persisted in taking grain from customers, an illegality which, in England, was known as "hanging up the cat." Only with time, farmers began to get smart. If a customer came to pick up his sacks when the miller was away, he did unto the miller what he was sure the miller had already done unto him. He took a bit of the miller's grain. It was the customer, in fact, who would call out at such a time if the two met, "Hey, Henry, I've taken up my meal, *and* I've hung up the old cat."

But not all millers were thought of as scoundrels. Most, in fact, were extremely diligent, independent

In the sixteenth century, post mills were used in England and on the continent of Europe to grind grain. This mill drawn in 1508 by Chapman and Millar, Edinburgh's first printers, was typical. It turned into the wind.

men with strong minds of their own, and often rather ingenious. It wasn't unusual for a miller to tie a string of tin cups to his mill's sails to wake him up if the wind started in the night, or to tie a rope to his blanket and attach the other end to the mill's sails. That way, a miller would often be literally rolled out of bed if the wind came up after he had gone to sleep.

Perhaps the best description of a miller's life dates from the eleventh century and is still applicable to the few millers that remain today. The English historian Alfred Hills suggests that a miller's qualities

are those of a sailor, and life in a windmill, buffeted by the wind, is not unlike that on board a ship. The miller is usually short, because he is jumping about all hours of the night instead of growing. He is strong enough to carry a sack of wheat on his back, yet wiry and active, constantly running upstairs to see that the grain is flowing to the stones properly, then down to test with his thumb the quality of the meal, then descending to the

The insides of an eighteenth-century Dutch windmill were hand-made from wood, often imported from America. Tightly fitted gears turned the shaft to grind grain, pump water, or make paper.

ground to push the windmill's tail around, as the wind draws into another quarter.

Like the sailor, the windmiller loves his mill, keeps it carefully and loyally in trim, and drives it skillfully. His cheerfulness is the more remarkable because he has to spend days of enforced idleness, when the wind drops, and everything stands still. Then in the evening, just as the other folks are putting on their jackets and knocking off for tea, the breeze springs up, and the miller sets his sails and works through the night. If the wind holds, he will run her for two days and a night without stopping.[4]

It was an established fact, however, that no matter how high the wind, millers never worked on Sunday —that is, if they wanted to continue to hold the religious respect of their clients. To make up the loss, they normally unfurled their sails and prayed for the great wings to spin from Sunday midnight to Tuesday evening, Wednesday morning to Thursday night, and Friday morning to Saturday midnight.

According to wind enthusiast Stanley Freese, when a windmill started up, the real excitement began.

The noise and motion, beginning with a little creak and shudder, quickly swells to a crescendo, gathering like a

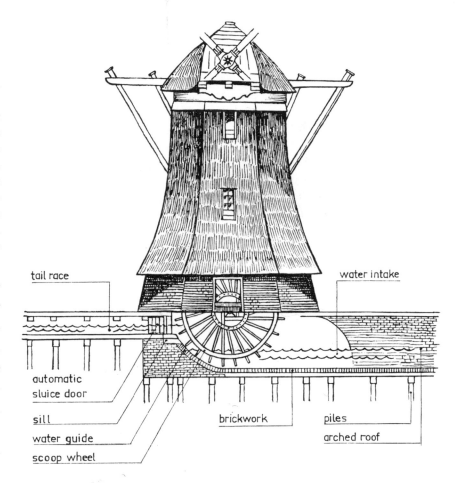

This drainage or polder mill was used in South Holland, and had an internal scoop wheel.

hurrying storm. . . . Creaking and swishing in the wind, the sails sweep round majestically, with a gentle "slap, slap" of the shutters as each sail comes down from aloft. . . . The wind is rising, and the miller seizes a weight from the reefing chain, thus lightening the load on the shutters and checking the gathering speed of the mill . . . the great runner-stone is already revolving with a rumbling, roaring note that fills the dusty air.

Big wooden cogs are meshing through their iron counterparts. . . . The huge sails, accelerating again in a rising wind, traveling 30 miles an hour at the tips, throw the mill from side to side as they catch the wind aloft, bringing every corner of the old mill to life . . . so that the great body is wrenched about with loud protesting cracks, shuddering uncomfortably under the strain; chains rattle and sack-traps bang as sack after sack goes up to the top of the mill. The damsel, clattering rhythmically . . . rises to an incessant noise . . . so that the miller shouts to make himself heard . . . the vibrations have, in fact, gripped the whole structure as the wind drives her furiously along.[5]

At times, in fact, the effect of the wind on the wooden structures which dotted the European landscape in profusion until the middle of the nineteenth century could be disastrous. One example was an incident which occurred in 1849 at the Barking Mill in England. It was reported that day that

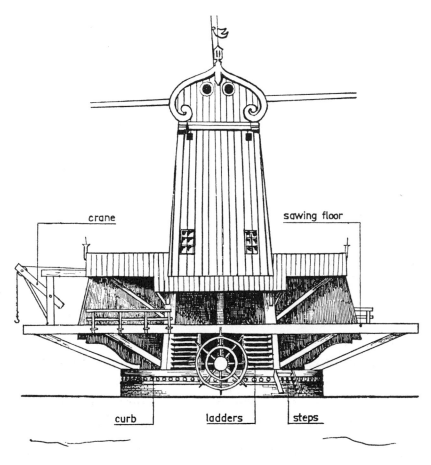

Windmills are able to perform many different tasks. The paltrok *sawmill was used in Holland.*

Dutch windmills were used for many purposes. This one, seen from the front and side, is a sawmill, a smock mill type, with a sawing floor and storage area. Blades turn inside.

The wind yelped about the countryside like a pack of angry dogs. It snarled about the mill, rattling the pitch pine scantlings and snagging at the door-latches: it snapped and retreated, leaving a damaged sail. A laborer was sent out to repair the breakage, and, as he was firmly astride the vane, the wind returned with such ferocity that the propeller broke, man and sail falling 66 feet to the earth. The man was dead, the sails shattered to matchwood.[6]

Windmill accidents continued to be a real threat to millers until the middle of the nineteenth century, at which time there was a new threat—the potential obsolescence of the miller. Nations which had formerly depended on windpower began to shift their allegiance to steam. England's Richard Trevithic, a Cornishman, had first demonstrated its effectiveness in 1805 when he drove a 70-ton steam powered barge down the River Severn. After 1827, when the first ship completely powered by steam crossed the Atlantic, the pressure for change increased.

For the Dutch, however, the transition was gradual. Windpower had long been the nation's greatest ally, and no one was anxious to abandon it.

3

Windmills in Holland

Blue and white Dutch tiles from Delft often depicted windmills.

Descartes put it simply: "God made the world, but the Dutch made Holland." But what he didn't point out was that without windmills, the Dutch might not have succeeded. From the start, inhabitants of this small country, often known as The Netherlands or the "Low Lands," faced a problem of drainage. In fact, up until 1000 A.D. Holland was barely habitable. The land was mostly below sea level and was in actuality a series of marshes crossed by a few sluggish streams, separated from the sea, or the "water wolf," as the Dutch called the North Sea, by a belt of dunes. Most of the inhabitants of the country lived on a series of earthen mounds. When floods came, as they inevitably did, thousands of people died. In the St. Elizabeth flood of 1421, for instance, 72 villagers were washed out to sea.

Finally, though, by the middle of the fifteenth century, a solution was found. Sections of land, called polders, were surrounded by high earthen walls, or dikes, to protect them from the sea. The dikes had

Windmills were everywhere in seventeenth- and eighteenth-century Holland. Many pumped water off the land. Others, such as these, ground farmers' grain. The sails were usually covered in canvas. "When you hear the first rustle of cloth, you set your mill into the wind," a modern miller says. "Then you pray. We work when the wind blows."

On the flat Dutch landscape, windmills gave grandeur to the works of artists, especially to Rembrandt van Rijn.

Jacob van Ruisdael delighted in windmills, too. This is a variety of stellingmolen, or a mill with a stage.

small holes in them to allow the water inside to drain out. Later, trap doors were introduced which permitted constant drainage, but could be closed if the outside water level became too high.

It wasn't until the fifteenth century, however, that the Dutch really progressed in their battle against the elements. By using powerful windmills they were able to keep the polders dry. The windmills provided the power to lift water out by the thousands of gallons, 24 hours a day, and dump it into other troughs where more windmills pumped it still farther away until eventually it was returned to the sea.

By 1608, the 10-foot-deep Bremster Lake had been emptied by 26 windmills. Subsequently, the Purmer, Wormer, and Herhugowaard Lakes were also drained. But the most startling reclamation of the age was the Schermer project, which required the work of 51 mills for four years. By the time the lake was dry, in 1634, Holland's land area had begun to resemble that of the country today.

Besides being functional, the mills added greatly to the beauty of the landscape. For painters, they

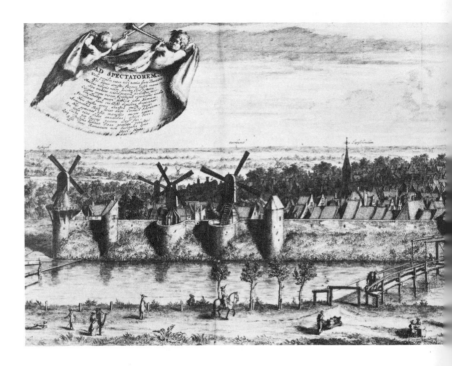

One of Holland's richest cities, Delft had many windmills in the sixteenth and seventeenth centuries. Built inside the walls for the citizens' convenience, especially when the city was attacked, the mills not only kept Delft dry, but they also ground the housewives' grain.

were major focal points on an otherwise flat Dutch horizon, where they stretched out by the dozens, their majesty and grandeur lending a backdrop of drama and excitement to fields of cows and acres of wheat. In fact, Rembrandt van Rijn, who was the son of a miller, derives the last part of his name from his father's malt mill "de Rijn," in Leiden.

Like all his fellow countrymen, the artist's love for the mills was enormous. At the height of Holland's devotion to the windmills, over 9,000 mills lined the dikes and canals which covered the land. The windmills' sails were attached to a central wooden axle, or shaft, inclined toward the horizon at an angle of about 10 to 15 degrees to best receive the curvature of the wind. The planes of the sails were placed obliquely to the plane of the revolution, and turned like a pinwheel in a nearly vertical axis when the wind blew in their direction.

The sails themselves were made of 30- to 50-foot-long wooden frames with canvas covering their lattice or framework. The rotation of the sails turned large, toothed gears, which could provide power for various

operations, including a millstone, a lumber saw, or even a rag chopper to make paper.

Of the eight basic types of windmills that can still be found in Holland today, the oldest are of the post variety, dating to 1300. These mills, called standard molen, are made so that the whole millhouse with its sails can be turned around its shaft and moved by a tail-post at the rear. The *wipmolen*, or hollow post mill, resembles the post mill but it is not as high and has a house that is more cubical. The prototype of the Dutch polder and drainage mill, the wipmolen usually has a substructure that is covered with thatch.

Other types of windmills can still be seen in Holland today. One of these is the tower mill with a stage, known as the *stellingmolen*. A very large, tall mill, it was often built on the ramparts of old towns and had a large circular stage halfway up with a

In modern-day Holland, only 900 of the country's original 9,000 mills still stand. Most need restoration. Here in six-teenth-century Heusden, three standermolen, or post mills, have been beautifully brought back to life.

This seventeenth-century engraving by Dutch artist Jan van de Velde is entitled "Summer." These standermolen date back to about 1300.

Icol Moolen

3

The post mill, or standermolen, is Holland's oldest type of
mill. A tail pole allows it to be moved to catch the wind.

Gort Moolen

2

The hollow post, or wipmolen, is the prototype of the Dutch
drainage mill. The miller usually lived inside.

Seem Moolen

A North Holland drainage mill, or binnenkruier, *has a cap which can be turned by the miller to face the wind.*

Meel Moolen

Perhaps one of the most picturesque of all Dutch windmills, the post mill is one of the simplest to operate.

Located near Groot Ammers, the cap of this bovenkruier, *or drainage mill, can be turned by a winch or handwheel.*

In a Vermeer-type farm setting in modern-day Holland, this stellingmolen, *or stage mill, continues to grind grain.*

handrail. Here, millers could reach the sails and turn the mill's cap in order to head it into the wind. Another type of windmill is the *bovenkruier*, or upper winder, which has a tail pole and handwheel at ground level, that permits its owner to steer it in the right direction to capture the wind.

Since Holland's windmills were ingeniously designed to fit the needs of the products which they produced, almost no two were ever alike. These dynamos of wood and brick and thatch were somewhat like a ship in that someone always had to be in charge to see that they were properly directed. Like the sea captain, the miller was never able to create the source of energy but was always striving to tame it.

The miller had to be strong, agile, and able to go without a night's sleep in order to take full advantage of a strong wind. He had to also be able to smell a wind 20 miles away, and be up and out to unfurl his sails in the light of the moon if necessary.

But at other times, a miller could be forced to spend days in idleness. Although he was never able to start the mill on his own, a miller would stop his mill

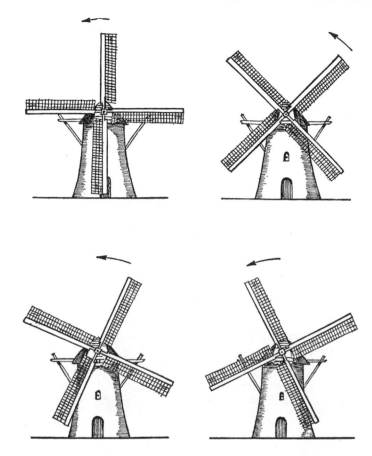

Over the centuries, millers adopted a sign language of their own. Windmills served as newspapers. The wings of the windmill above left say, rest for a short period; above right, rest for a long period; below left, celebration; below right, mourning. A mill's sails turn clockwise.

usually to transmit a message to his neighbors. Over the centuries, millers adopted a sign language of their own and their windmills served as newspapers. By positioning the wings of a windmill, millers could alert the entire countryside to an important event. For example, when a baby was born, the wings were set in a "coming position," an almost completely vertical-horizontal position. A slight twist further clockwise into the "going position" told of death. A mill, in fact, could remain this way for six weeks, unless there was work to be done. Then, if possible, the body of the mill was turned in the direction of the deceased's house, sharing its grief with the family.

But when there was happiness in the polder, the mill burst forth in all its glory, especially for a wedding. Then, the windmill was set in a diagonal position, or made to "stand pretty." The lattices of its sails were woven with garlands of flowers, and decorated with hearts, trumpets, and stars made of tin that sparkled in the sun. On top of each upper arm, cartouches with the bride's and groom's initials stood tall, while from the top of the mill, the Dutch red-

Large and tall, this stellingmolen, *or stage mill, is built to catch the wind above other buildings' roofs.*

white-and-blue tricolor flapped in the breeze.

In more recent history, Holland's windmills have communicated more serious information. As Catholic millers during the Reformation had signaled by sail when and where a mass would be held, so millers during World War II alerted members of the Dutch underground to enemy movements as well as Allied needs. Many an English and American pilot whose plane had crashed in a polder was helped out of the country by the Dutch underground, alerted to his whereabouts by the tip of a miller's sails.

Long before the war, however, the Dutch had become bent on abandoning the windmills which had provided them with energy for five centuries and had enabled them to keep their land dry and their stomachs fed. With the discovery of the steam engine in England in the nineteenth century, the Dutch, too, began to shift their allegiance from windpower.

In Kinderkijk, Holland, 19 windmills still operate. Drainage mills with wing spans from 93 to 97 feet, their sails turn Saturday afternoons in July and August.

After five centuries of deriving their energy from the wind, the Dutch shifted their allegiance in the middle of the nineteenth century. The steam engine rapidly took over.

One of the biggest problems millers face is determining which direction the wind has shifted without going out of doors. Small weathervanes such as this one provide the answers.

Because they were at first reluctant to put the preservation of their polders in the hands of a new-fangled contraption, the Dutch polder boards delayed the introduction of the steam engine for a while. But the decision to reclaim the Haarlemmermeer (the Big Harlem Lake) changed their minds. The project was sufficiently monumental that only the use of steam engines would make it feasible. In 1848 they ordered three 400-horsepower steam engines from England, and put the machinery into action quickly so that in four years the lake was completely drained.

Historically, the completion of the Haarlemmermeer project marked the real start of Holland's switch to steam and abandonment of the wind as a source of energy. With locomotives puffing their way through the countryside, bellowing forth clouds of smoke, people began to think of themselves as behind the times if they were not using steam power. Soon, pumping stations sprouted up throughout the land, their boiler houses, engine houses, and coal sheds lining the landscape. Finally, polder boards gave in and began to make the change from wind to steam.

Here in the Schermerpolder, six Dutch windmills survive out of an original 50. During World War II, the country had over 1,400 mills. Now, there are about 900. The Dutch Windmill Society struggles to save as many as it can.

Modern-day miller Johan Jansen works a windmill at Brede-voort. One of approximately 160 professional millers, many of whom work part time in the 250 Dutch windmills now in operation, Jansen grinds grain on weekends as a hobby.

Before long, windpower was a thing of the past. The construction of one steam pumping station could replace five, six, seven, or eight windmills. Where once a windmill's sails had graced the sky, now smoke stacks rose up like exclamation points. Sometimes, the mills would be merely abandoned, left to fend for themselves against the elements. Others were stripped of their sails and turned into homes. Many others were torn down.

By the beginning of the twentieth century, with the introduction of electricity, windmill demolition increased on a large scale. In 1913, the decision to drain the 17-foot-deep Hazerswould Lake brought

Thatch made from reeds continues to cover the sides of many windmills in Holland. Few thatchers remain, however. Therefore, many mills must wait a long time to regain their original beauty.

about the construction of three electric pumping stations and the destruction of 15 windmills. In 1923, the board of the polder De Honderd Morgen of Wilde Veenen demolished seven mills, and the Eendrachtspolder board did away with eight more mills.

No demolition project rivaled that on the Schermerpolder, in which 50 mills were torn down. Their destruction in 1927, after 300 years of service, caused an uproar among windmill preservationists, members of the growing De Hollandsche Molen, the Dutch Windmill Society. This group lobbied continually for the restoration and maintenance of Holland's remaining mills, and was instrumental in obtaining for windmill owners federal and local government funds of up to 90 percent of a windmill's restoration costs. Today the Society's hard workers are justifiably proud that approximately 950 windmills still stand in Holland.

The fact that the 1,440 Dutch windmills that still existed in World War II were used to keep the polders dry during the German occupation and helped preserve the nation is an important argument advanced today by the Dutch Windmill Society for the preser-

Located near Rotterdam, "The Swan" is owned by Baroness Van Till and used as a weekend cottage. It dates back to 1702.

vation and restoration of the nation's remaining mills.

According to Cees van Hees, executive secretary of the Society, the cost of a mill's restoration is between $15,000 and $75,000. Obviously, without government support few people could afford such an undertaking. "But, the trouble is that it simply isn't enough to restore a mill," van Hees states. "It has to be run, too." The mills are subject to destruction by the wood borer worm, which infests mills that are no longer in operation. Vibrations caused by the turning sails apparently repel the borers.

Today, about 60 polder mills and 20 corn mills work full time in Holland, with another 50 polder mills and 55 corn mills functioning part time. Of the total, roughly 40 percent are privately owned, while the rest belong to polder associations and local mill preservation societies.

Of the country's remaining unrestored windmills, many are in demand as residences. Approximately 2,000 people live in windmills and there are another 1,500 on a waiting list to purchase them or rent them from polder societies. "With the high rents in cities,

The interior of "The Swan" near Amsterdam serves as a comfortable two-story weekend house for Baroness Van Till.

Neglect, fire, rain, lightning—both man and nature have been the enemies of Dutch windmills down through the centuries.

This once-proud mill is an example of what can happen when mills are abandoned and retirement sets in.

Restored mills, such as this one lived in by Melleken Muysken and her husband at Schermerhorn, Holland, are a joy to owners.

people have discovered the joys of living within the sails of a mill, and often at very reasonable rents," says Piet Myksenaar, president of the Dutch Windmill Society. To learn how to operate their mills, millowners can become members of the Guild of Volunteer Millers. At present, there are an estimated 160 professional Dutch millers, many of whom work only part time in the 250 Dutch windmills now in operation, but there are 240 apprentice millers now in training.

Arie Butterman, 21, who is in charge of "De Schoolmeester," or the Schoolmaster, is among the group of instructors who devote their Saturdays to training these new millers. In charge of turning the sails of Holland's last paper mill to pulverize rag for the Van Gelder Paper Company, which still has a request from artists for mill-made watercolor paper, Butterman had his miller's license by the time he was 17 years old.

Melleken Muysken, known by colleagues as the "molen moeder," or "mill mother," is one of eight female Volunteer Millers in Holland. Mrs. Muysken's

At "De Schoolmeester" or the Schoolmaster, Holland's last paper mill at Westzaan, miller Arie Butterman weighs rags.

interest in mills triggered her enrollment in the guild's course in 1970. Shortly before, she and her husband, a nuclear engineer, and their children had moved to the Schermer polder into "de Valk," or the Falcon, a "binnenkruier" or inside-winding drainage mill, one of a number of mills in Holland large enough to be lived in.

Having herself passed the guild's stiff examination, Mrs. Muysken screens would-be millers today. Every two weeks, she journeys to a different part of the country to administer the examination to candidates for the miller's degree.

Among the professional millers, Jacob Kaal is one of the best known. In charge of "de Zoeker," or the Seeker, at Zaandijk, a region 30 minutes north of

In Holland, the Guild of Volunteer Millers teaches men and women of all ages the art of working restored Dutch mills. There are 240 apprentice millers enrolled in Guild classes throughout the country. The Dutch people are becoming more aware of windmills as part of their national heritage.

In Zaanse Schans, north of Amsterdam, Jacob Kaal and his wife care for "de Zoeker," or The Seeker. Built in 1672, it is the only working peanut oil mill left in the world. A mustard mill and a saw mill are also still in operation in this industrialized zone. All the mills in Zaanse Schans welcome visitors.

Amsterdam where only a half dozen mills remain out of an original 100 or more, Kaal operates the world's last peanut oil mill, owned by a nearby oil factory. Built in 1672, the Seeker presses tons of peanuts each year and processes 700 liters of oil a week.

Kaal, a lifelong miller, can also report on one of the industry's greatest hazards—fire. "I've seen three mills burn. It's horrible, but fascinating," he admits, honestly. "First the body burns to a skeleton. The arms start whirling furiously; then they slow down, wave backward and forward for awhile, as if pleading for mercy, and suddenly the whole structure collapses."

It was such an experience that another of Holland's well-known millers, Arie Berkhout, remembers well. "A lot of the wood in this mill," he said, patting the timbers of "de Roode Hert," or the Red Deer, in Audorp, outside Alkmaar, "was in my father's mill

At the end of the day, millers furl the canvas sails that cover a mill's wings. When covered, the wings, turned by the wind, operate the mill's internal mechanisms.

A complex system of wooden gears, cogs, ropes, and hatches makes up the internal mechanism of a Dutch windmill.

which burned down. It was salvaged. And, like a Phoenix, the mill rose up again."

Berkhout is one of Holland's last full time millers who is self-employed and earns his entire living from milling grain. A family would be difficult to support on a miller's earnings, according to Berkhout, who lives with three unmarried sisters in a house 20 feet from the mill.

"To really capture the wind, a mill must be high, on a raised piece of land," he explains. "Otherwise, there isn't the free flow of air that is necessary for uninterrupted power. However, we don't always need as strong a wind as many people mistakenly believe." A strip of metal called the leading board, invented in 1946, is placed along the front of each of the Red Deer's sails. It functions like a sailboat's jib sail, and enables the sail to turn in only a slight breeze. The canvas itself is moved by the incomplete vacuum created on the leeward side. The wind whistling through the opening between the leading board and the sail maximizes the vacuum and makes the windmill's sails turn.

The sails of the Red Deer whirl at the rate of 80 times a minute. Lifting the grain bags on one level for grinding, then running down a level to fill them with the finished flour, the miller listens constantly for the flap and snap of the canvas, the thump and moan of the wood gears.

"The tiniest difference in sound signals the need to be alert," Berkhout cautions guild students, who hang on his very word.

> A miller is a bit like a sentry. He has to be constantly watching and listening, ready at his post to go into action if anything goes wrong. The parts that go into a mill are very sensitive to excess friction. A fire can start, or meshing can be worn away very quickly if you aren't right on top of things.

As in most mills in Holland, each piece of wood in the Red Deer is imported from a foreign country. "This is a Douglas fir, shipped to Holland from America in 1748," Berkhout explains, caressing the mill's

An eighteenth-century rendering of a drainage mill from "Groot Volkomen Molenboek" reveals a complex interior.

Windmills still stand in many towns in Holland. The mills provide a picturesque focal point of the flat Dutch landscape.

The van Malsens are farmers who live in a restored drainage mill, or post mill, the oldest type of windmill in Holland. He is a graduate of the Guild of Volunteer Millers which teaches novices the art of working windmills.

main shaft. "And the gears on that shaft, the one over there, are boxwood, probably brought here from England. The other gears, over there, are made from vinegar wood found in the Pyrenees."

But of all the parts of the mill, none is as important as the millers themselves. According to Cees van Hees of the Dutch Windmill Society,

> We are always being asked to supply underdeveloped countries with windmills as a source of cheap energy. But the thing the inquirer inevitably forgets is that it takes people to run the mills. Even if there was the money to build the structures themselves, and they cost far more than most inquirers realize, without [experienced] millers to run them and millwrights to repair them, they could quickly become white elephants.

In 1952 a Dutch foundation was established for the purpose of investigating the possibility of using windmills once again to supply energy. Two old windmills were modernized and began to produce electricity but they were deactivated in 1972 because of their inefficiency. Not only did their output not cover their operational costs, but it was learned that

A working windmill is noisy, with hatches opening and slamming closed, wooden gears grinding, and ropes and pulleys whirring.

one of the old-fashioned type of windmills can meet only one-millionth of the country's entire need, according to the Dutch Windmill Society.

Despite these pessimistic statistics, however, William E. Heronemus, University of Massachusetts engineering professor, has urged Holland as well as the United States to build a network of gigantic windmills off their coastlines. "Holland could achieve a high degree of independence from fossil fuels like oil, coal, and gas—and their attendant woes—by practicing modern technology windpower in the same way as America must now do," he counsels.

Speaking of his network of windmills as "wind barrages," Heronemus describes what tomorrow's power plants might be like.

> The barrages would resemble a suspension bridge with towers at least 600 feet high. There would be two pairs of suspension cables and between them would be bolted

Today's high cost of electricity has caused scientists to reconsider windpower as an alternate energy source. But it takes time and money to develop modern windmills.

> a structural grid that rotated about a central vertical axis. Twenty wind generators would be placed in this grid. Each of these rotating windmill clusters would have a maximum generating capacity of 400 kilowatts and would be placed about half a mile from each other.[7]

The energy produced would, in turn, be used to convert ocean water into hydrogen and oxygen, Heronemus explains. The hydrogen would be shipped ashore to be combined with the oxygen in fuel cells to produce electricity, or burned pure as a fuel. Since it produces a hot flame that emits only water vapor and no soot or particles, hydrogen is considered one of the cleanest types of fuel.

> Each mile of wind barrage could produce at least 24 million kilowatts of electricity a year. Barrages about 500 miles long could produce about 12 billion kilowatts a year. This is the output expected from two one-thousand megawatt nuclear plants achieving 65 percent reactor availability.[8]

The revolutionary Stirling Engine, being developed by the N. V. Philips Company of the Netherlands at Eindhoven, could be used as a conversion device, Heronemus adds. Invented by the Rev. Robert Stir-

This miniature drainage mill stands only five feet high. Small mills are used to keep pasture lands free of marshes. The tail keeps the mill headed into the wind.

ling in Scotland in 1817, the Stirling Engine has been developed as one of industry's quietest, cleanest, and most efficient multi-fuel heat engines. The vast quantities of oxygen produced by the windmill could also be utilized to treat sewage, produce large amounts of pure drinking water, and depollute rivers.

Convinced that his windpower system, complete with its storage subsystem, could produce electricity more cheaply than the conversion plants of today or the planned nuclear-energy systems of tomorrow, Heronemus suggests that the Dutch wind barrages could be adapted to the whole European Economic Community, at least to augment the hydroelectric power already available.

At one stage in history, Western man was willing to work for centuries on individual buildings, content with the belief that one day the end product would be to the glory of God, even if he would never see it himself. It is time to think again like the Cathedral architects did in their time and devote our energies and capital to projects that will last as long as the sun will shine and the wind will blow.

I would think that the same kind of ocean engineering

ingenuity that created Holland would find the erection of a contemporary windpower system a relatively easy task.[9]

Whatever role windpower is to play in Holland's future, as well as that of the rest of the world, one thing is certain: The Dutch are determined that the windmills which exist in Holland today will remain for centuries to come. Although they were obsolete for over a hundred years, Dutch windmills have had a comeback. Once more, their sails have begun to turn. For awhile on the Dutch island of Texel, one windmill was lighting lamps, running television sets, and heat-ing homes. Until it was damaged by a storm in 1973, the mill added energy to the local power station, and provided enough energy to keep 50 families in elec-tricity. The only problem was that the revolution of the sails caused TV interference and therefore the mill couldn't be operated at night.

"It's ironic," one islander says. "Today, we com-plain about a little fuzziness in our TV reception. Five hundred years ago, we fussed about water in our liv-ing rooms. The windmill met our needs then, and it will again today. Only mankind has to give it a chance!"

4

Windpower in the United States

Lloyd's Mill, Brooklyn, N.Y., was destroyed by fire in 1868.

The first windmills used in the United States were introduced by the early Dutch settlers. Two of the earliest windmills, dating back to 1622, overlooked the Hudson River in the town of New Amsterdam, now New York, and were used for grinding wheat. Across the East River in a farming community called Breukelen, later Brooklyn, another wind machine ground the early settlers' corn into flour.

In 1650 English settlers in Jamestown, Virginia, also introduced the local Indian population to the wonders of harnessing the wind. But the heaviest concentration of windmills in the United States always remained in the north. Today, in fact, the greatest collection of seventeenth- and eighteenth-century windmills in the Western Hemisphere is in Suffolk County, New York, on Long Island. Because there were few swift streams to supply water power, early residents of Long Island looked to the wind for their energy needs. Through preservation and good fortune, ten of these English-style "smock" or "petti-

coat" windmills, with rotating caps, can still be seen —at Gardiner's Island, Shelter Island, Wainscott, Bridgehampton, Water Mill, Shinnecock, and East Hampton.

Because they were costly to build and cumbersome to operate, European-style windmills never came into widespread use in America; for the most part, the early settlers did not find them a practical source of energy. However, in 1854, Daniel Halliday revolutionized the entire concept of windpower. Realizing the need of ranchers to provide water for their families and livestock, he invented an easily constructed tower topped by a light wheel fitted with automatic mechanisms to break its speed when the wind increased and to furl it out of action when a tank of water was full. Later, Halliday's windmill was used to generate enough electricity to meet the needs of a small house. Some historians believe that Halliday's

This New Jersey windmill was typical of those in the area in the early nineteenth century. Many windmills were also operating on Long Island. Lower Manhattan can be seen in the background.

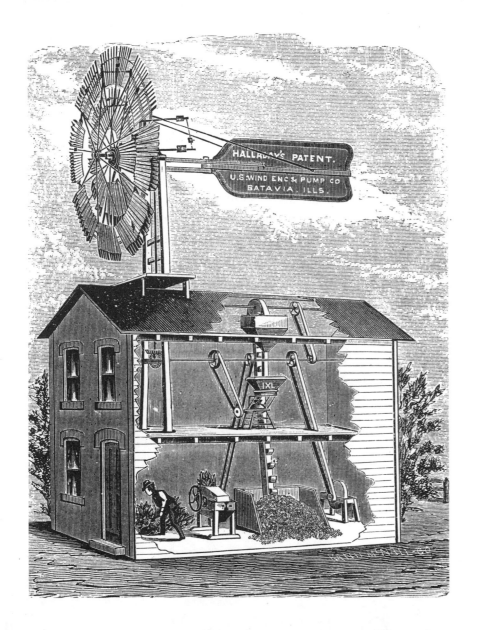

invention, soon copied and improved upon by others, was a major factor in the rapid settling of the West. It was certainly a blessing to the men who built the railroads. Windmills lined the course of the railroad tracks as they were laid westward. Without water to quench their thirst, railroad laborers wouldn't have lasted long under the sweltering sun.

By 1900, windmill production in the United States had exploded into a ten-million-dollar-a-year operation with over 20 companies competing for the farmers' and ranchers' dollars. In Texas and Wyoming and almost every other state west of the Mississippi, a windmill turning in the breeze rapidly became a common part of the landscape.

The demand for tower windmills (which produced 1.4 billion horsepower-hours of work a year, the same amount of energy that is produced today by burning 11.8 million tons of coal) was much greater than even

In the late nineteenth century, windmills populated the American plains. Most were used for irrigation. This one, though, was used for shredding tobacco leaves.

the best market forecaster of today would have dared hope. From 1880 to 1935, an estimated 6,500,000 windmills were sold in the United States—a proliferation that caused one traveler to write that "the vast American prairie is practically alive with them."

In the mid-twentieth century, however, windmills slowly began to decline in use. In 1958 sales for the Aeromotor Company of Chicago had peaked with the firm capturing 80 percent of the 100,000 tower windmills sold that year in the United States, but by 1970 sales were down to 5,000. Under President Franklin D. Roosevelt, the government had introduced rural electrification to the nation in the forties. Electricity at that time became more reasonably priced and more reliable than the wind, especially for areas with low altitudes. Therefore electricity met with steadily increased popularity.

The Heller-Aller Company of Napoleon, Ohio, another windmill manufacturer, founded in 1884, suf-

An advertisement for a type of windmill that was popular in the early part of the twentieth century.

The New Elgin Marks

STRONGEST SINGLE GEARED MILL

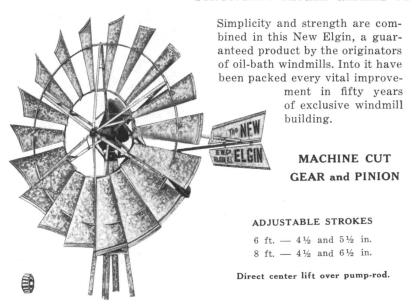

Simplicity and strength are combined in this New Elgin, a guaranteed product by the originators of oil-bath windmills. Into it have been packed every vital improvement in fifty years of exclusive windmill building.

MACHINE CUT
GEAR and PINION

ADJUSTABLE STROKES

6 ft. — 4½ and 5½ in.
8 ft. — 4½ and 6½ in.

Direct center lift over pump-rod.

STRONGEST WIND WHEEL

Crimped wheel blades catch more wind—pump more water in the lighter breezes—and with the extra heavily braced arms, give greater strength to withstand storms. Stream lines of the semi-steel head offer no flat surfaces for cyclones or blizzards. This main casing is in three sections, the edges of which are tongued and grooved and fit so tightly together that neither dust nor water can get through nor oil leak out.

The steel vane and its angle steel frame operate without springs or chains that cause trouble in more cheaply made mills. Governed by a weight ball and arm, the moving parts of which are inside the head, this mill automatically applies the wide steel brake band on a brake drum at the base of the wheel hub. This hub is in one piece and screws onto the shaft. The drum can be quickly replaced without removing wheel or any parts except brakeband.

Large 2-Stroke
Machine Cut Gear

For decades, Aeromotor and Eclipse windmills were a common sight on American farms. Used primarily to pump water for cattle, these mills were manufactured by the thousands.

fered a similar setback. Going from sales as high as 4,000 windmills in the 1920s, the company received requests for only 375 windmills in 1970, although the next year, helped by mention in *The Whole Earth Catalogue*, company sales rose to over 1,000.

This increase in sales, according to the company president, was attributable to the increased interest in windpower on the part of a constantly growing number of Americans, especially young people. The United States, because of its growing awareness of ecology and the limited supply of fossil fuels, may well, in fact, be paying more attention to the potentialities of windpower than any other country in the world right now.

Other alarming statistics have also contributed to the reawakening of interest in the United States in the potential of windpower. With less than 6 percent of the world's population, the country consumes more

Jacob's Wind Generators were built in the United States from 1930 to 1950. This mill, atop a modern tower, is a survivor from an era when windmills were a common sight across the country.

With the introduction of rural electrification, wind-powered water mills fell into disuse on most American farms.

than a third of the total fuel used on the planet. And, in the last 100 years, the United States has increased its consumption of fuel twentyfold.

The result, scientists explain, was that total U.S. energy consumption in 1970 was the equivalent of 80 slaves working for each of us to maintain our modern, efficient way of life. And it is expected that Americans' consumption of electricity will double between 1970 and 1980, and almost quadruple by 1990.

"If we were the slightest bit sane," one wind enthusiast says, "we'd be working night and day to capture windpower more effectively and save humanity at the same time."

Fortunately, many people are doing just that. By the year 2000, windpower could yield 5 to 10 percent of the United States' electricity, or 1.5 trillion kilowatt-hours of electricity annually, an amount equal to the total electricity consumed in the country in 1970, according to a report prepared jointly by the National Aeronautics and Space Administration (NASA) and the National Science Foundation.

As a result of this and other favorable reports, federal financing for windpower research will be up to $12 million in 1976. Among the fifty windpower projects currently supported by the government is a $500,000 contract awarded by the National Science Foundation and NASA to two industrial firms for preliminary designs of large wind systems. The two contractors, General Electric Company Space Division and Kaman Aerospace Corporation, will examine modern versions of windmills at sizes that generate 100 kilowatts for use by small communities or farm cooperatives, to three megawatts for possible connection into the power networks of large utility companies.

According to NASA, a three-megawatt windmill would be the largest ever built. Its roto-blades would, in fact, be about 200 feet in diameter and each windmill would produce enough electricity to supply 100 to 200 homes.

The National Science Foundation is also planning to invest $30 million in wind research in the next five years. Already it has spent nearly $1 million to begin to construct the 100kw Experimental Wind-Turbine Generator near Sandusky, Ohio. Scheduled to be 160 feet tall and to have 125-foot-diameter blades, the windmill, being managed for the foundation by NASA's Lewis Research Center in Cleveland, Ohio, will be able to supply enough electricity for 30 homes, it is hoped. Joseph Savino, head of the NASA team entrusted to build the government structure, believes that positive results in windpower research will encourage utility companies to construct wind-generating machines across America in a system of power plants.

Further windpower research is also going on at another NASA research center at Langley Air Force Base in Hampton, Virginia. The Langley vertical axis windmill, which is being developed there, looks more like a piece of modern metallic sculpture than a windmill. Located on top of a two-story building, about 50 feet off the ground, the windmill is based on a design patented by French inventor G. J. M. Darrieus in 1927. The machine's two blades, able to turn in almost any wind, have a 14-foot diameter and are made of balsa wood covered with fiber glass, and the 15-foot vertical shaft is made of aluminum tubing.

Looking like half an egg beater, the two curved blades are attached at top and bottom to the shaft. This circular combination sits on top of a simple gear system and a generator that converts the wind into energy.

The Langley windmill does have a major obstacle, however, one which its followers, under the supervision of Dr. John D. Buckley, the project engineer, are hard at work to overcome. Although it is self-starting in a wind of 12 mph, it will only accelerate to about 13 rpm, no matter how much the wind velocity increases. If assisted initially by hand pushing, however, it can attain a speed of 65 rpm, and then the rotors rapidly accelerate to a free-running speed of about 213 rpm.

According to a study made by the Canadian National Aeronautical Establishment in 1970–1972, the established power output for a 15-foot-diameter windmill similar to the Langley vertical axis model is 1.3 horsepower, or one kilowatt, in a 15 mph wind velocity.

"Our greatest advantage is simplicity," says Dr. Buckley, who feels the Langley windmill may cost

Vertical axis wind turbines are under research by NASA in Hampton, Va., Sandia Laboratories in Albuquerque, N.M., and by the National Research Council of Canada in Ottawa. They are based on 50-year-old French and Finnish designs.

from $500 to $1,000 to buy and install and meet the needs of one family. "More conventional windmills require a tail vane or other means to keep them headed into the wind, and those with horizontal axes demand more complicated gear mechanisms which decrease efficiency and increase costs."

At universities, research into windpower is also forging ahead. At the University of Oklahoma, engineers are testing a windmill with a new type of generator. The rotor doesn't have to turn at a constant speed to produce power; therefore, the machine's blades will be able to turn freely as the wind increases. The device is the brainchild of Tom Chalk, a St. Cloud, Florida, inventor and aircraft mechanic. The Chalk windmill, an airfoil that looks like a bicycle wheel, is patriotically colored red, white, and blue. With forty-eight blades, it can convert more than 50 percent of the wind passing through it into usable energy. Equally important, its light weight allows it to spin in breezes which won't budge other windmills.

With a 15-foot-diameter wheel which weighs 120 pounds, versus conventional 16-foot-multiblade windmills which usually weigh over 1,000 pounds, the Chalk airfoil is able to spin on its own. The inventor's smaller model is equally compact. Chalk's eight-foot wheel weighs 25 pounds, compared to most manufactured windmill wheels of the same size model which weigh about 370 pounds.

At first, in fact, scientists were reluctant to believe Chalk's breakthrough. Dr. William Hughes of Oklahoma State University in Stillwater came to Florida to test Chalk's claim that his windmill could increase by 20 percent the efficiency of most typical farm windmills. The results of the tests were sufficiently impressive that Hughes left Florida with three of Chalk's models to test them in the Middle West.

Eventually, Chalk intends to use the spinning rim of his windmill's wheel, where the surface speed is extremely high, as the armature of an electricity generator. In the meantime, he estimates that if the machine is hooked up to a water pump and a 60-foot well, it could easily double or triple the 400 gallons of water pumped per hour in a 15 mph wind by today's average 8-foot windmill.

The SST (Super Speed Turbine) designed by Thomas Chalk of St. Cloud, Fla., is being manufactured by American Wind Turbine, Inc., in Stillwater, Okla. Its prototype is painted a patriotic red, white, and blue.

Funding, Chalk explains, was the problem which he found the hardest to solve. It is a complaint registered by government and private wind enthusiasts everywhere. The inventor's next step, he says, is to explore the possibility of the manufacture of his design in small "do-it-yourself" kits and ready-to-run units for homes and also large, high-output units suitable for small communities, large farms, and factories.

A research program at Oregon State University started in late 1971 under the sponsorship of four Oregon People's Utility Districts is also at work on windpower. The team is investigating wind fields in coastal, offshore, and inland regions of the Pacific Northwest. Dr. Wendell Hewson, Chairman of the Atmospheric Sciences at Oregon State University, is especially optimistic about the windy Columbia River Valley. In stressing the tremendous power behind the

Thomas Chalk was an electronics service technician before devoting full time to developing his SST.

One of Thomas Chalk's early designs for the SST stands next to a competitive power source. When efficient wind-powered generators are mass produced, their prices will be much less than they are today.

At Princeton University, Thomas E. Sweeney, Senior Research Aeronautical Engineer, developed a wind generator called "Sailwing." The prototype in Princeton colors, orange and black, is being tested on the campus airstrip. Grumman Aerospace Corp. is also testing "Sailwing."

wind, he points out that a 30-mph wind yields eight times as much power as a 15-mph wind. He envisions windmills in the Columbia River Valley producing 2,000 to 5,000 kilowatts of power, pumping water up over dams and back up the river, thus keeping the water at a high level. Thus it would be possible to keep hydro-generators going even in winter when the rivers are usually low, and energy needs for home heating are at their peak.

"Windpower would allow us to use existing dams and not further endanger the environment," Dr. Hewson states. "To raise [the level of water in] a reservoir only a few feet would make all the difference in hydro-generation."

While government agencies and many universities are busily investigating the prospects of producing effective energy from windpower, private industry has also turned its attention in this direction. The Grumman Aerospace Corporation is currently testing a small wind generator, called a Sailwing, for possible production and sale. The 300-pound windmill was designed by Thomas E. Sweeney, Senior Research Aero-

nautical Engineer in Princeton University's Aerospace and Mechanical Sciences Department. The device has a 25-foot-diameter rotor blade and an aluminum mast. According to Sweeney, it could be manufactured to sell for between $3,500 and $4,000 and could be capable of operating a 7-kilowatt generator.

"Excessive wind pressure has always been a windmill problem because of the very high drag forces it creates at high speeds," Sweeney says. "Windmills tend to fall down or become damaged. We expect that Sailwing's adaptation of airplane structural technology will minimize this problem."

Made of dacron, the Princeton windmill takes on a familiar airfoil curvature when the wind blows. At rest, the stretched fabric lies in a flat plane.

Also hard at work harnessing the wind is a team of five young people on a farm in Wisconsin. Windworks, as the group is called, is financially backed in part by inventor and philosopher R. Buckminster Fuller, and under the direction of aeronautical engineer Hans Meyer. The group has designed and built several small wind generators, some of which have been tested on Fuller's island in Maine, but it is especially proud of one device which can be constructed for about $200 with easily obtainable materials.[10]

Near Albuquerque, New Mexico, Robert Reines and the Integrated Life Support Systems Laboratories have also been at work. They have created the world's only dome structure powered entirely by wind and solar energy. Since they installed their first wind generator in 1972, they have added two more for additional electricity plus a solar heat collection system. Prototype I, as the dome is called, thus has its own independent supply of heat and hot water.

Not all wind research is taking place on land, though. For example, Pennwalt Corporation, whose principal business is the manufacture of light and fog signals to mark offshore drilling platforms, has been applying its thinking to the nation's current energy

At Windworks in Mukonago, Wis., Hans Meyer and associates are investigating a variety of windmill designs. Their work is partially funded by R. Buckminster Fuller. He has had experimental windmills on his island in Maine.

Jessica and Jack Dickson are homesteading in Maine with the help of a Swiss-made Elektro windmill. Wind genera- tors of this kind will be costly until mass production and increased demand bring prices down to realistic levels.

problem. The company bought 10 French-made Aero-watt Windmills at $4,000 apiece, and mounted them on platforms in the Gulf of Mexico to generate electricity to power the markers. Whether the windmills remain or not will be determined by their cost savings.

Research and experimentation with windpower has not been limited to the efforts of the government or private corporations or groups. Individuals as well are interested in the economics of windpower. Artist Neil Welliver with his wife and three children from Lincolnville, Maine, received an estimate from the Central Maine Power Company of $10,000 to bring electricity from the main road to their home. Flabbergasted at the price, Welliver promptly sent off a letter to Australia to order a Quirks Wind Plant. It cost $3,000 to buy and erect, and Welliver believes it was worth every cent. Today his studio and home are powered by free electricity from the wind.

Henry Clews, entrepreneuer, has imported both Australian and Swiss wind generators for sale in the United States.

Painter Neil Welliver and his family live on a mountain top in
Maine. It was too costly to have electrical wires brought up
from the main road. Two Dunlite wind generators and storage
batteries supply their electrical needs.

One of Henry Clew's Swiss-made Elektro windmills blends in beautifully with sapling birch trees in East Holden, Maine.

Encouraging progress in windpower has also been made by Henry and Etta Clews, of East Holden, Maine. The Clewses' home was so far from "civilization" that they knew from the start that power-company-provided electricity was out. "The lines were just too expensive to bring in," the 31-year-old aeronautical engineer says. So, the Clewses also wrote to Australia and imported a 2,000-watt Dunlight windmill for an initial investment of $2,800. Later, a second windmill was ordered, this time a $7,000 Swiss-made Electro windmill of over 4,000-watt power.

By attaching their windmills to an alternator, the Clewses can convert direct current (DC) immediately to alternating current (AC), from which they run most of the appliances in their house. Excess energy is stored in 20 lead-acid batteries that hold four days' worth of power.

So far, the system has been able to "provide power enough for eight 75-watt light bulbs, radio, TV, stereo, electric typewriter, blender, toaster, vacuum cleaner, power saw, electric drill, as well as for a 1/3 hp deep-well water pump."[11]

Windpower is a derivative of solar energy, a fact that is often overlooked. The U.S. government appropriates funds each year for research on solar energy.

The Clewses were swamped with as many as 1,000 letters of inquiry a month as news of their independence from the Bangor Hydro-Electric Company spread and so the couple founded the Solar Wind Company, the exclusive sales outlet in the United States for the firms which manufactured the two types of imported windmills that they use. To date, they have sold close to a dozen systems, making enough money to live on and provide them with funds for further research into windpower.

"Other than for 20 hours in the last six months when we've had to turn to our gasoline generator, the wind has met all our energy needs," Henry Clews says. Yet he cautions, ". . . don't be deceived that the wind generates less expensive electricity than that which is available to most people who live near a power line."[12]

At the present time, electric companies charge 3¢ to 5¢ per kilowatt hour, excluding installation costs, which for Clews amounted to $10,000. Assuming a 10-year life for his storage batteries and a 20-year life for his windmills, Clews estimates his power costs about 15¢ per kilowatt hour. Aside from the economics, though, it is the freedom he and his family have and the conservation they are practicing that pleases Clews the most.

Mass-produced wind-generated electricity may be more cheaply produced, however, than individual units, advocates believe. The optimistic William E. Heronemus, professor of civil engineering at the University of Massachusetts in Amherst,[13] since the early seventies has urged the construction of huge wind generators to provide practically all the United States' electricity needs. At one time a nuclear supporter, Heronemus now is fearful that nuclear power is dangerous. He therefore urges the use of windpower to his growing following of students, government officials, and industrial leaders.

He is especially anxious to oversee the construction of a network of windmills on top of huge floating buoys ten miles off the New England coastline which would generate electricity in mammoth quantities. Records kept 15 years ago by the Air Force on offshore New England winds show that there is ample

William E. Heronemus, professor of civil engineering at the University of Massachusetts, envisions windpower as more than an "alternate" energy source. If properly developed, windpower could supply a high percentage of our energy needs, he feels.

velocity to generate electricity year round.

Another Jules Verne–type dream which Heronemus envisions is a network of 300,000 giant windmills, each 850 feet tall, spaced as closely as one per square mile, across the Great Plains from Texas to North Dakota. Fifty-foot-diameter propellers, similar to those used on aircraft only larger, would capture 59 percent of the wind's power, 8 percent more than has ever been captured to date. He predicts that with such a Herculean system in operation, one trillion kilowatt hours a year of power could be extracted from the wind. While the windmill system wouldn't be the exclusive solution to the nation's energy needs, it would contribute a major amount to the 1.75 trillion kilowatt hours of electricity that the United States generates annually.

Although Heronemus's ideas may sound a bit visionary, they are no more farfetched than a project

Forrest Stoddard at the University of Massachusetts prepares the blades of an experimental windmill. Students across the country are taking classes in windpower.

that was undertaken in 1934 at Grandpa's Knob in Vermont.

Pioneered by the Central Vermont Public Service Corporation, this project was one of the boldest experiments in windpower ever undertaken anywhere in the world. The corporation erected a gigantic, 1,250-kilowatt wind-powered generator with stainless steel blades which was visible for 25 miles around Rutland, Vermont. The idea had come from Palmer Putnam, an engineer who wanted a small wind-driven electric generator for his home on Cape Cod. Realizing that the commercial type available at the time was not large enough for his needs, Putnam began extensive research. He dug into books to see what the French, the Dutch, the English, and other people of the world had done to capture the wind. Putnam concluded from his research that in order for windpower to be economically feasible, it had to be undertaken

William E. Heronemus at the University of Massachusetts envisions tall, off-shore wind barrages to capture the stiff ocean breezes. The towers would be beyond the horizon.

on a large scale for a large number of people. He then interested the S. Morgan Smith Company of York, Pennsylvania, builders of turbines, to underwrite his project.

The plan called for all the electrical current produced by the windmill to be used as backup power to pump water behind a local dam so that when the wind wasn't blowing hard enough, customers of the Central Vermont Public Service Corporation weren't without power. The company, a subsidiary of the New England Public Service Company, had agreed to cooperate since it relied solely on water power and was delighted with the prospects of diversifying and improving its performance.

Finally, after looking over more than 50 sites on which to build the project, one was selected. The site, a 2,000-foot-high mountain, was purchased from a

Grandpa's Knob in Vermont was the largest, most successful windpower plant ever built. Operating in the early forties, it supplied thousands of homes with electricity.

farmer who insisted it didn't have a name, but that it was merely "Grandpa's." Because of the mountain's peculiar shape, it came to be known as Grandpa's Knob.

Experts from the California and Massachusetts Institutes of Technology, Stanford University, and Harvard conferred on the Grandpa's Knob Experiment, and finally a 110-foot-tall windmill with a two-blade propeller nearly 175 feet in diameter with each blade weighing 8 tons apiece was set up.

On October 19, 1941, the windmill began to operate. For the next three-and-a-half years, in winds sometimes as high as 115 mph, the turbine generated as much as 1,500 kilowatts of electric power. Then in 1943, the machine was shut down for two years because it required repairs that were difficult to complete during the war. On March 3, 1945, the wind turbine was set in operation again, supplying thousands of Vermont homes with energy.

Twenty-three days later, on March 26, after three weeks of perfect service during which time 61,780 kilowatt-hours had been generated in 143 hours and 25 minutes of operation, Grandpa's Knob, the largest, most successful windpower plant to have existed in the world even to this day, stopped operating. Hidden cracks in one of the blades had caused it to fly off, and repairs were costly. Because of this disaster and continued wartime scarcities and labor shortages, the $1.25-million Grandpa's Knob Experiment was abandoned. But the experiment had proved that man could build a practical machine which would generate electricity in large quantities by means of windpower, according to Dr. Vannevar Bush, former president of the Carnegie Institute and head of the Office of Scientific Research and Development during World War II.[14]

For Yankees blessed with a combination of economy and nostalgia, Grandpa's Knob is a constant reminder of something else in these times of inflation. "There's still plenty of wind up there and the price hasn't gone up one cent," says Charlie Gibson of Brownville, Vermont.

5
Windpower in the Rest of the World

A wind-powered carriage designed in Italy in 1648.

All over the world, from ancient times up until the present, men have made attempts to harness the wind. There is hardly a nation on earth that has not profited at some point from windpower.

Although the windmills that Don Quixote futilely tilted at still exist in Spain, probably the best-known windmills in Europe, outside of Holland, are Greece's ancient windmills on the island of Mykonos. Of enormous size, with light-rigged sails, they may well have been turning 3,000 years ago at the time of Odysseus and his sailors. Smaller windmills also abound in Greece. According to Professor Paul P. Santorini of the National Technical University in Athens, about 10,000 small, primitive windmills pumped water on the mainland and on the Greek islands as recently as 1961. Today the number is considerably less because of increased rural electrification.

In New Delhi, India, in 1954, the government organized a symposium on Wind Power and Solar Energy in conjunction with UNESCO's Committee on

The best-known windmills outside of Holland are on the Greek islands. Mykonos is the most famous for them.

Arid Zone Research. As a result, in 1955, India planned to erect 30,000 windmills by 1960 to provide energy to irrigate the arid regions from Saurashtra in the northwest to the Madras in the southeast. To date, however, the proposal for turning Indians from hoof power to windpower has produced few lasting results. Reluctance to change among country people lies deep, government authorities admit. Nevertheless, with the construction of a 25-foot-diameter sail-wing windmill in 1973 near Madurai, Tamilnude State, and the successful testing of two types of wind-electric generators, able to produce 12 volts/250 watts, in the early 1960s in Bangalore, it is possible that the Indians may come to accept this new technology. Moreover, as the cost of animal feed increases, oxen may become more expensive to maintain than the cost of alternative types of energy, such as windpower.

Experiments in Morocco with windpower took place in Mogador when the Moroccan Coal and Wind Research Society erected a wind machine in 1949 with a 58½-foot sail spread. Linked to the town's

Almost every country in the world has utilized windpower at some time. From Persia to England, from Spain to China, the windmill has helped man for centuries. New windpower research is underway in many countries around the globe today.

main electricity generating plant as supplementary power, it worked well, but it was not introduced elsewhere in the country. Moroccan officials felt that the windmill's high construction cost and therefore its high cost of energy output did not warrant further windmill research and development.

Even the Russians have contributed to man's knowledge about windpower. In 1931, Soviet engineers constructed a 100-foot-diameter wind turbine in Yalta. Driving a 100-kilowatt generator, the unit reportedly produced 279,000 kilowatt-hours of electricity a year and supplemented the output of a steam-power plant in Sebastopol, 20 miles away. Further research continued at Balaclava, where Russian scientists with the Central Institute of Wind Energy set up a 97-foot-diameter windmill, reported to have achieved a 100-horsepower output in a wind velocity of 26 feet per second.

In Denmark as well, prior to the end of World War II, a network of small windmills generated a capacity

A tall tower windmill was the first constructed in the Holy Lands. Its wings turned in the city of Jerusalem.

of 100,000 kilowatts of electricity. At the end of the war the government realized that most of the nation's electricity from 1940 to 1945 had come from the wind and therefore launched a windpower research program. The project was abandoned shortly thereafter. An inexpensive supply of surplus hydroelectric power became available from Sweden. Today, quite a few of the old Danish windmills continue to dot the landscape after nearly half a century with no maintenance of any kind, but only a few generate any electricity.

In Scotland, in the 1950s, a windmill was operated by the North Scotland Hydro Electric Board on the remote wind-swept Orkney Islands. But after eight years, the project was dropped in favor of what today is recognized as a premature hope of unlimited power from nuclear fission.

Further south, at St. Albans, England, in 1955, still another windmill turned freely in the wind. Known

By the year A.D. 1000, records show that windmills were in operation in many European countries.

as a "turbo-prop" with no gear train to hold its sails down, the windmill's hollow blades were propelled by centrifugal force, causing air to shoot out through their ends. A semi-vacuum thus having been created inside the apparatus's 100-foot-high pedestal, air rushed in through its ports, and on the way upward, turned a turbine that drove a generator. Again, however, public disinterest prevented continuation of the project.

Interestingly enough, England was once second only to Holland in the number of its windmills, and the country's artists and painters delighted in their presence. John Constable, like Rembrandt, grew up in a mill and depicted others in Dedham, East Bergholt, Dorset, and Sussex. In fact, he died while painting a windmill on one of his canvases.

Attesting to the abundance of windmills in England, William Cobbett, a resident of Ipswich, recorded that at one time

Renowned English architect Inigo Jones designed this classic Georgian windmill at Chesterton, England.

In addition to the pyramids and the Sphinx, ancient Egypt also contained many windmills. This one stood near Cairo in 1881. It is thought that windpower was first tapped in Persia before the birth of Jesus.

This West Indian horizontal windmill was used for grinding sugar cane in the production of rum for export both to the United States and Europe. The design is identical to windmills in use in Spain under the Muslim rule.

the windmills on the hills in the area are so numerous that I counted, whilst standing in one place, no less than 17. They are all painted or washed white, the sails are black . . . and their twirling together added greatly to the beauty of the scene, which, having the broad and beautiful arm of the sea on the one hand and the fields and meadows studded with farm houses on the other, appeared to make the most beautiful sight of the kind that I ever beheld.[15]

Before long the landscape here and elsewhere in England was sadly altered. Statistics indicate that where there were once 50 working mills in the Chatham and Rochester districts of England, today there are none. And while as late as 1926 there were 48 working corn mills in East and West Suffolk, only four, operating part time, now remain.

In fact, of the estimated 30,000 windmills operating in the late nineteenth century in Denmark, Germany, England, and the Netherlands, which produced an equivalent (in mechanical power) of 1 billion kilowatt-hours of electricity, only a few thousand are still standing today.

Of these, the majority are of far greater interest to tourists than to local utility companies.

6
Prospects for the Adoption of Windpower

*Scientists today are designing windmills different
than any ever envisioned.*

Throughout the world windpower dreams have all
suffered from the same weaknesses. First of all the
cost of windpower was no less, and often greater,
than power produced by fossil-fueled plants. Second,
no satisfactory system for storing energy had been
devised for those days when the wind didn't blow.
Therefore, it was assumed that windmills would have
to be backed up 100 percent by alternatively
fueled energy plants during those periods when they
couldn't operate. And, finally, everyone had come to
assume rather prematurely that all currently used
forms of energy, including windpower, would soon
be made obsolete by the introduction of nuclear
power. As it is, however, the United States today
derives eight times as much energy from burning
wood as from fissioning uranium.

This reluctance to consider windpower as an energy source may be about to change, however, as
fossil fuel prices skyrocket. In fact, in Germany a return to the use of windpower has begun already at

the School for Naval Architecture at the University of Hamburg where Wilhelm Prölss has designed what he calls a Dyna-Ship. After spending two decades trying to discover the reasons for the decline of the sailing ship, Prölss determined it was because they couldn't be navigated quickly enough from low wind to higher wind areas. With improvements in global weather forecasting and navigational instruments, he reasoned, this problem has been lessened. And by taking advantage of modern aerodynamic improvements, sails could also trap a good deal more of the wind's energy, Prölss figured.

As currently designed, Prölss's twentieth-century clipper ship will carry masts 200 feet high with no lines or shrouds. The yards in the square-rigged system will be made of curved stainless steel fitted with tracks so that the sails can roll out from the center of the mast. Prölss has, in effect, designed a continuous airfoil from the top of the mast to the bottom, the angle of which will be set by turning the mast hydraulically via remote control on the bridge.[16]

Tests conducted at the University of Hamburg have proved that North Sea winds can be sufficient 72 percent of the time to propel the Dyna-Ship at speeds up to 20 knots an hour. This is a marked improvement over a top speed of 13 knots for most nineteenth-century clipper ships. Furthermore, for a full-scale 17,000-ton model, fully automated, fuel consumption is estimated to be only 5 percent of that of an ordinary freighter. The ship will, however, have to be powered by oil when entering harbors or in those areas of the world where there is little or no wind.

Engineers at the university also report that the Dyna-Ship's low operating and construction costs, plus its large cargo hold, will allow owners a 30 percent higher return on their investment. Rudolf Zirn, a Bavarian lawyer and environmental activist, was convinced by these reports and commissioned the construction of the first Dyna-Ship, to be used for exploration. Its cost is estimated to be about 5 million dollars. A Lübeck shipbuilder named Friederich Beutelrock has also ordered a Dyna-Ship to be tested for efficiency on international freight runs.

The West Germans are also conducting windpower research on the island of Sylt in the North Sea where a team of wind enthusiasts—two Swiss engineers, a French electronics expert, and two West German scientists—has designed a windmill and operated it successfully since 1973. The Sylt Island windmill is expected to be able to produce 70 kilowatts of power at an investment of about $45,000. The team points out that the initial investment would be 20 to 30 percent less if the windmill were mass-produced.

As presently designed, the German windmill is capable of supplying five families with electricity and heating, and can obtain power from winds as slow as 4.5 mph. Using two rotor blades that turn in opposite directions and an electric generator mounted on the axis between the two rotors to take advantage of a high relative speed between them, the windmill's design has eliminated the need for gear wheels to con-

There are experimental windpower projects all over the world. On the West German island of Sylt, a windmill is capable of supplying five families with heat and electricity.

vert the slow rotational speed of the rotor into the much faster speed necessary to drive the generator.

This cost saving and increased efficiency make the Sylt Island windmill as efficient as earlier energy-generating windmills and already competitive with fossil fuels. An added advantage is that it can convert more than 60 percent of the wind's force into electric power, compared with a 30 percent conversion rate for a good conventional windmill, and the research team anticipates increasing the machine's efficiency to as high as 90 percent.

Thus far, $190,000 has been spent on the West German windmill, which is expected to last 20 years and produce energy at a cost of 2.7¢ per kilowatt-hour. Already, the team has blueprints for a windmill that could produce 230 kilowatts. They also have designed a 30-kilowatt windpowered generator that could easily supply a household's needs.

Tackling the problem of energy storage, perhaps the most nagging issue currently facing windpower researchers, the group is currently experimenting with heating stones and heating water in special tanks, as well as using storage batteries.

To date, no European firm has expressed any interest in working with the men to develop their ideas still further; the only definite interest that has been shown has come from enterprises in the United States and the Mongolian Socialist Republic, and they have not yet followed through on it. The limited amount of interest that has been shown in the Sylt Island windmill is puzzling to the team, especially since the device uses current technology and could be mass-produced almost immediately.

In view of the problems still to be worked out, is it really foolish to look to windpower for part of our world's future energy needs? No more so, according to some scientists, than depending on a pile of dead plants, the ultimate source of all our current fossil fuels.

Wilson Clark, author and consultant for the Environmental Policy Center, realized several years ago the link between energy and society. "The real energy crisis for our civilization is one of survival," he says. "We cannot begin to replenish the stored energy of the earth quickly enough to meet future energy use levels."[17] The connection between man and the power behind his television set, his bedside light, or his automobile is no longer simply a utility bill or a gaso-line-company credit card. Instead, it is now a matter of how long will the earth's fossil-fuel energy last? How long will it be until the light bulb flickers and goes out? How long until the car sits idle in the garage, starved to death by lack of fuel?

With 75 percent of the current U.S. energy con-sumption dependent on the earth's dwindling fossil fuel and the expectation that U.S. electricity needs alone will double by 1980, time is rapidly running out.

The crisis is no less severe throughout the rest of the world, and government leaders and utility-com-pany executives can no longer afford to delay the in-troduction of new resources that will meet growing

A fifteen-foot-diameter vertical axis wind turbine under-goes tests at Sandia Laboratories in Albuquerque, N.M. This design is often called an "egg beater" windmill.

energy needs. As prophets of new forms of power raise their voices every day to broadcast more loudly the need for vigorous energy research and development in all possible areas, including windpower, the growth of the earth's population alone should testify to the urgency of the need. Between 200 and 300 million people had settled on the earth at the time of Jesus. By 1650, the figure had jumped to 500 million. It had taken 1,650 years to double the earlier population. But by 1850, only 200 years later, the earth was home to one billion men and women, and today the period of time it takes for the population to double is even shorter. Thirty-five years from now there will be two times as many mouths to feed as there are right now!

Along with these new citizens of the world, there will be more houses to heat in winter and cool in summer, more transportation systems to run, more assembly lines to automate . . . all of which take power. And this power must come from somewhere.

There are, of course, those forces who argue against the potential of windpower, and often for very self-serving reasons. One large oil company, discoverer of the Prudhoe Bay oil field on the North Slope of Alaska, ran a TV ad in 1974 depicting a windmill with sails turning in the dusk and light streaming from one of its windows. "Back in 1915, 3,000 windmills helped light up the country of Denmark," a voice told viewers. "America could generate electricity the same charming way. All we'll have to do is keep wasting our natural stores of energy. When it's all gone, we'll just turn on the windmills. A great idea, 'til the wind dies down." With that the windmill's sails stopped turning, the lights inside went out, and the viewer was left to hear a great deal of swearing in Danish.

The same year another company, engaged in the manufacture of earth-moving and coal-mining equipment, placed an ad in several major American business magazines. In it, a young man pointed to a windmill. "The perfect energy. Clean, cheap, and can't foul up the environment," he said to his older companion.

"But, it can't meet today's needs," was the reply.

"Too bad about windmills. They just aren't a practical solution to our energy dilemma," the ad claimed, and concluded with a statement praising coal.

Where does the truth lie? Are the advocates of windpower being too utopian, or are its adversaries merely reluctant to admit to the value of something so infinitely available?

R. Buckminster Fuller supports the latter point of view. "Great corporations have not as yet ventured into the field of windpower because wind energy has not seemed to be monopolizable over a pipe or wire," he says. "Enterprise can be rewarded, however, in greater magnitude than ever before by producing and renting world-around wind-harnessing apparatus—following the models of the computer, telephone, car rental, and hotel-servicing industries.

"Windpower permits humanity to participate in cosmic economics and evolutionary accommodation

For generations, scientists and designers have attempted innovative windmill constructions. This windmill, entitled "Romeo and Juliet," was designed by Frank Lloyd Wright, and built at the Hillside Home School in Wyoming Valley, Illinois.

without in any way depleting or offending the great ecological regeneration of life on Earth," Fuller contends.

Stewart Udall, the former U.S. Secretary of the Interior, wrote of the potential of windpower in 1970.

> Windmills are much, much more than relics. They are symbols of sanity in a world that is increasingly hooked on machines with an inordinate hunger for fuel and a prodigious capacity to pollute. Ecologically, the windmill is one of the few perfect devices. It harnesses a completely free resource to pump water or generate electricity under conditions that respect the laws and limits of nature.
>
> Like waterwheels and sailboats, windmills have a Zero Environmental Impact (ZEI). If we are to meet the challenges, inventors and technicians will have to pay homage to windmills. They'll have to build machines that use, not abuse, the unearned gifts of nature.[18]

The World Meteorological Organization conservatively calculated that the wind's ultimate energy potential could provide a yearly harvest of 20 billion kilowatts of power, a figure much less than others estimate. This puts the available wind energy in the Northern Hemisphere alone at 80 trillion kilowatts.

The remarkable fact is that the technical understanding necessary to build large windpower generators is available. French engineer Louis Vadot, chairman at the United Nations' sessions on windpower generation at the New Energy Conference in Rome in 1961, stressed that

> It is now generally agreed that the design of wind power plants with capacities ranging from the lowest levels to far beyond 100 kilowatts no longer presents any fundamental problem.
>
> In the field of calculation and theoretical aerodynamics, our present knowledge is sufficient to be usable in a more or less routine way and without need to be on guard against surprises.
>
> In the field of engineering, the record of achievement shows that here, too, we are on firm ground. In the case of very large machines, there are, of course, still some small imperfections of detail, but it is rare to find any branch of activity in which such a small number of prototypes (100-kilowatt and above) have produced so few failures. It is very encouraging.[19]

What seems to be one of the biggest deterrents to putting windpower to work is mankind's general obsession with new inventions rather than the refinement and adaptation of past ones. Gary Soucie, in *Audubon Magazine* suggests that

> If windpower were a new and untried idea, if it weren't an old-hat idea and a Persian old-hat at that, the utilities might be falling all over themselves to try it out . . . Nothing alarms a technofreak so much as to suggest that he look backward or toward the inscrutable East.
>
> Someone—I wish I could remember who—once said that at the brink of an abyss, the only progressive step is a backward one. Just think of the socio-technical revolution that might overtake us if we started looking backward—not just to windmills, but also to solar heaters, steam and electric cars, passenger trains, houses built with more regard for climate than for architectural fashion, products designed for use rather than for throwing away.[20]

In answer to pessimists' complaints that windpower is interesting but impractical, William E. Heronemus suggests that, "In the United States, today, 'impractical' usually means that something isn't fancy enough to appeal to our ideas of high technology and flamboyant life style."

In the end, however, even the greatest skeptics of windpower must admit that only trial and error, not apathy, will produce the new sources of energy necessary to solve the world's energy crisis. If windmills are thought to be anachronistic, let us call them aerogenerators, if necessary, and begin seriously to consider this free, clean, limitless power source so obviously worthy of full-scale investigation.

Notes

1. Don Guy, "An Investigation of Wind Power," *Yankee*, March 1974, pp. 84–97.
2. Wilson Clark, *Energy for Survival*. Anchor Books, Garden City, N.Y., 1974, p. 268.
3. Rex Wailes, *The English Windmill*. Routledge and Kegan Paul Ltd., London, 1954, p. 153.
4. Robert Thurston Hopkins, *In Search of English Windmills*. London, 1931, pp. 33–34.
5. Stanley Freese, *Windmills and Millwrighting*. At the University Press, Cambridge, 1957.
6. Frank Brangwyn and Hayter Preston, *Windmills*. Dodd, Mead, and Company, New York, 1923, p. 38.
7. *Holland Herald*, vol. 8, no. 8, 1973, p. 8.
8. Ibid.
9. Ibid.
10. Plans are available by writing to Windworks, Box 329, Rte. 3, Mukwonago, Wis. 53149.
11. Henry Clews, *Electric Power from the Wind*. Solar Wind Company, East Holden, Maine, 1973, p. 20.
12. Ibid., p. 14.
13. William E. Heronemus, "The United States Energy Crisis: Some Proposed General Solutions," presented before a joint meeting of local sections of the American Society of Mechanical Engineers and the Institute of Electrical Engineers, West Springfield, Mass., Jan. 12, 1972. Also, "Windmills," *Environment Magazine*, vol. 15, no. 1, January/February 1973.
14. "A Promise in the Wind," *Yankee*, March 1974, p. 96.
15. Stanley Freese, *Windmills and Millwrighting*. At the University Press, Cambridge, 1957, p. xiv.
16. James McCawley, "Return of the Tall Ships," *Rudder*, 1971, pp. 29–31, 70–72.
17. Wilson Clark, "Interest in Wind Is Picking Up as Fuels Dwindle," *Smithsonian*, Nov. 1973, p. 70.
18. Stewart Udall, *The New York Times*, 13 February 1971, p. 27.
19. Louis Vadot, *New Sources of Energy*, Proceedings of the Conference, Rome, Aug. 21–31, 1961. United Nations Publications Sales No. 63.1.41 E/Conf 3/8, 7:188, 1964.
20. Gary Soucie, "Pulling Power Out of Thin Air," *Audubon*, vol. 76, no. 3, May 1974, pp. 81–88.

Appendix

Companies Currently Engaged in Research, Manufacturing and Marketing of Wind Generators

DESIGN-RESEARCH-DEVELOPMENT

Boston Wind Co.
   307 Centre St.
   Jamaica Plain, Mass. 02130

Kaman Corp., Kaman Aerospace Div.
   Bloomfield, Conn. 06002

Research & Design Institute
   25 Holden St.
   Providence, R. I. 02908

MANUFACTURER

Aerowatt S.A.
   37 Rue Chanzy
   75—Paris lle
   France

Bucknell Engineering Co.
   10717 E. Rush St.
   S. El Monte, Ca. 91723

Dunlite Electrical Co.
   Div. of Pye Industries
   21 Frome St.
   Adelaide 5000, Australia

Dyna Technology, Inc.
   Ecological Science Corp.
   Sioux City, Iowa 51102

Elektro G. M. b. H.
   Winterthur
   Switzerland

Lubing Mashinenfabrik
   Ludwig Bening
   2847 Barnstorf
   P. O. Box 171
   West Germany

105

Natural Power, Inc.
New Boston, N.H. 03070

Northwind Power Co.
Warren, Vt. 05674

Zephyr Wind Dynamo Co.
Box 241
Brunswick, Me. 04011

MARKETING

Energy Alternatives, Inc.
69 Amherst Rd.
Leverett, Mass. 01054

Enertech Corp.
Box 420
Norwich, Vt. 05055

Pennwalt Corp.*
P. O. Box 18738
Houston, Texas 77023

Solar Wind Co.**
RFD 2, Bar Harbor Rd.
E. Holden, Me. 04429

Vermont Energy Products
Box 849
Lyndonville, Vt. 05851

Northeast Utilities
Newington, Conn. 06111
Participating with Kaman Aerospace Corp. to
design up to 3,000 kw generators.

*U.S. distributor for Aerowatt
**U.S. agent for foreign windmills and Dyna Technology of
Sioux City, Iowa

Bibliography

Brangwyn, Frank and Preston, Hayter. *Windmills*. New York: Dodd, Mead, and Company, 1923.

Clark, Wilson. *Energy for Survival, the Alternative to Extinction*. Garden City, N.Y.: Doubleday, Anchor Press, 1974.

Clews, Henry. *Electric Power from the Wind*. East Holden, Maine: Solar Wind Company, 1973.

Freese, Stanley. *Windmills and Millwrighting*. Cambridge: At the University Press, 1957.

Handbook of Homemade Power, The Mother Earth News, c/o The Register and Tribune Syndicate, Inc., 715 Locust St., Des Moines, Iowa 50304.

Hopkins, R.T. and Freese, S., *In Search of English Windmills*. London: Cecil Palmer Publishing Company, 1931.

Livingstone, Richard N., "The Search for Alternative Energy," *The New Englander* 22, no. 8 (December 1975): 24–30.

Meyer, Hans. "Wind Generators: Here's an Advanced Design You Can Build." *Popular Science* 201, no. 5 (November 1972): 103–105.

Putnam, Palmer Cosslet. *Energy in the Future*. New York: D. Van Nostrand Co., 1953.

————. *Power from the Wind*. New York: Van Nostrand, 1948.

Reynolds, John. *Windmill and Watermills*. New York: Praeger Publishers, 1975.

Spier, Peter. *Of Dikes and Windmills*. New York: Doubleday, 1969.

Stokhuyzen, Frederick. *The Dutch Windmill*. New York: Praeger, 1970.

Vince, John. *Discovering Windmills*. Aylesbury, England: Shire Publications, 1973.

Wailes, Rex. *English Windmills*. Lond: Routledge and Kegan Paul, 1954.

————. *Windmills in England*. London: Architectural Press, 1948.

ADDITIONAL SOURCES OF INFORMATION

Alternative Sources of Energy, Route 1, Box 36B, Minong, Wisconsin 54859.

Henry Clews, Solar Wind, R.F.D. 2, Happytown Road, East Holden, Maine 04429.

Electrical Research Association, Cleeve Road, Leatherhead, Surrey, England.

William E. Heronemus, Department of Civil Engineering, University of Massachusetts, Amherst, Massachusetts 01002.

De Hollandsche Molen, 9 Reguliersgracht, Amsterdam-C, Netherlands.

McGill University, Brace Research Institute, P.O. Box 400, Ste. Anne de Bellevue 800, Macdonald College, Province of Quebec, Canada.

National Aeronautics and Space Administration, Lewis Research Center, Cleveland, Ohio 44135.

New Mexico State University, Las Crucis, New Mexico, offers a course in Wind Milling: instruction and training in the repair, installation and maintenance of waterpumping windmills.

Wind Energy Bibliography, Windworks, Box 329, Route 3, Mukwonago, Wisconsin 53149.

Wind Energy Utilization, Technology Application Center, Univertisity of New Mexico, Albuquerque, New Mexico 87131.

Windpower Digest, Jester Press, Bristol, Indiana 46507

Index

SOLAR CANADA

(A Division of DE Ltd., Est'd. since 1922)
4776 Wyandotte E., Windsor, Ont. N8Y 1H7
SOLAR ENERGY SYSTEMS AND PRODUCTS